APR '98

From Childhood to Adolescence

From Childhood to Adolescence

Including "Erdkinder" and The Functions of the University

MARIA MONTESSORI

SCHOCKEN BOOKS • NEW YORK

First English edition 1973

Copyright © 1948 by Maria Montessori
Copyright © 1958 by Desclée de Brouwer
Copyright © 1973, 1976 by Schocken Books Inc.

Translated from the French by
The Montessori Educational Research Center

Translation revised by A. M. Joosten,
Director, Montessori Training Center of Minnesota

Library of Congress Cataloging in Publication Data

Montessori, Maria, 1870–1952.
From childhood to adolescence.

Translation of De l'enfant à l'adolescent.
1. Montessori method of education. 2. Child study.
I. Title.

LB775.M72513 1976 371.3 75-34878

Manufactured in the United States of America

WE ARE VERY happy that this book, *From Childhood to Adolescence*, is being published by Schocken Books Inc. The Association Montessori Internationale is now actively joining with Schocken Books to promote the works of Maria Montessori in the English language. We hope that this book will be followed by others illustrating various aspects of the Montessori approach to education as a help to life.

MARIO M. MONTESSORI,
General Director
Association Montessori Internationale

Contents

FOREWORD   vii

PUBLISHER'S NOTE   xi

1. *The Successive Levels of Education*   3

2. *Metamorphoses*   9

3. *The Moral Characteristics of the Child from Seven to Twelve Years*   17

4. *The Needs of the Child from Seven to Twelve Years*   23

5. *The Passage to Abstraction—the Role of the Imagination, or "Going Out," the Key to Culture*   33

6. *Water*   43

7. *Some Chemistry Experiences*   59

8. *Carbon in Nature*   67

9. *A Few Ideas of Inorganic Chemistry*   77

10. *A Few Ideas of Organic Chemistry*   83

11. *Conclusion*   93

APPENDICES

A.   *"Erdkinder"*   97

B.   *Study and Work Plans*   111

C.   *The Functions of the University*   123

     INDEX   137

Foreword

DR. MARIA MONTESSORI'S NAME and work are still far too often associated only with the development and education of very young children, particularly with those of the so-called preschool child between two and one-half and six years of age. Even the most superficial acquaintance with Dr. Montessori's work could easily show the error of such an exclusive association. There is no doubt that during the whole of her long life and work she called on adult society (not the educational world only) to discover and recognize how truly fundamental the earliest years of childhood are; how the child, during those years, lays the foundation for his or her (therefore also our) life and being. There is no doubt either that Dr. Montessori's work with young children laid the basis for not only her educational, but also her social campaign for the recognition of the human and therefore social rights of children.

But one of the first outgrowths of this work was precisely Dr. Montessori's attempt to assist children during the second stage of fundamental development, from about six to ten or twelve years of age. Characteristically, as had already been the case when she started her first "Casa dei Bambini" (Children's House) in Rome in 1907 at the request of Edoardo Talamo, her decision to continue her work with older children was a response to a request made by others:

It was in 1911 that my friend Donna Maria Maraini Guerrieri Gonzaga wanted to lay the first basis for a private experiment, free from all trammels, to find out whether it would prove possible to continue the educational approach which had proved successful among very young children, with older children also. (Dr. Maria Montessori, Preface, "The Advanced Montessori Method," Vol. 1).

What would later be called, by others, the "advanced Montessori Method" therefore goes back to quite an early date, to hardly more than four years after the first "Children's House" was started. It can hardly have been accidental that this experiment was undertaken at the time that a group of children had completed their first stage of development with the help of a "prepared environment." Ever since, the number of Montessori environments for children over six years of age has grown and spread. They are found in several European countries as well as in America and Asia.

Dr. Montessori wrote her first book on this development in 1916—*L'Autoeducazione nelle scuole elementari*; the English translation was called *The Advanced Montessori Method* by the first publisher. Many years later, in 1948, there appeared, almost simultaneously, the French (original) edition of *From Childhood to Adolescence* and *To Educate the Human Potential* (Kalakshetra Publications, Madras, India). These publications deal with far-reaching developments of the Method and go well beyond the corework described in *The Advanced Montessori Method*, vols. I and II. The French book, of which this volume is a revised translation, was largely based on lectures given by Dr. Montessori at her International Training Courses in England and Holland during 1936–1939. The Indian publication is also largely based on lectures given during Dr. Montessori's stay in India from 1939–1946, but also on practical experiments carried out there by her and by her son, Dr. Mario M. Montessori, during that period. After World War II, separate training institutions were set up; among them the International Center for Montessori Studies at Bergamo (Italy) deserves special mention for its continuing pioneering work. Such "advanced training" is also given in a few other places in Europe and in October 1976, the Washington Montessori Institute intends resuming it in the United States. Meanwhile, Italian and German translations of the present book have also appeared and others are in preparation.

From Childhood to Adolescence is unique among the other Montessori books dealing with these developments as it also contains two chapters on education during adolescence and one on Dr. Montessori's views of the function of the university. In the early 1930s attempts had already been made in Holland to continue Dr. Montessori's approach to education with children from twelve years of age until the end of secondary (higher) education. Later other institutions for secondary Montessori education were started in France, and, after the war, in Italy and Germany. Dr. Montessori's own plan, first published by the Association Montessori Internationale (A.M.I.) just before the war, goes well beyond anything so far done and still awaits an opportunity to be implemented experimentally and practically.

These very brief historical notes would not be complete if we did not at least mention that Dr. Montessori also gave thought and attention to man's development from conception through birth to about two and one-half years of age and to the help that should be offered during that period. The Montessori Method, then, covers the whole of human development and expresses both what children had revealed to her and her own "intelligence of love," which urged her to respond to the needs of human development and help others to do so as well. Shortly after World War II a training institution was established in Rome to prepare its students to work with expectant mothers and their children from birth to two and one-half years of age. Practical work with remarkable results has been done in this area, particularly in Italy.

Montessori's recognition that development proceeds through successive, distinct periods—each having its own marked psychological and physical characteristics—is now accepted by many psychologists. Most conventional education, however, has lagged behind and does not utilize this insight in either its organization or approach, both of which remain basically uniform in all types of traditional schools. Nor is the insight implemented in the home to any significant degree. Sufficient attention is still not given to the essential unity of the human personality. This is evidenced by the lack of methodological continuity between pre-primary, primary, and secondary schools (not to speak of institutions of higher learning); between home and school, and between both of these and extramural activities and formal organizations like the Scout Movement. Dr. Montessori's method of education is, perhaps, still the only one that implements this insight practically as well as theoretically, the only one also that developed "organically" from its central effort to assist, not mold, the human being in its course of development. While giving full recognition to the characteristic needs of the human person during each of the stages of development, it no less explicitly recognizes the essential unity of the individual.

From Childhood to Adolescence offers examples. It is not a textbook. It is intended to help us build a new vision and perspective, it invites us to follow man-the-child into the new world he opens to us. It challenges us to try to pave the ways that help him explore and realize his world, to develop it and himself. While a great deal of practical work has been done and great results have been shown in the second period of human development —from six to twelve years of age—we can only hope that soon this too can be said for the third period of development —adolescence. It is a period in many respects as fundamental and critical as the initial period, beginning with birth. Dr. Montessori expected revelations from the adolescent perhaps even greater than those she experienced working in the Children's House. She truly believed that insights of adolescents, which lay waiting to be discovered, might well contribute to a general "human rehabilitation" of our adult world and society, as well as help provide solutions to problems of education at this stage that no one can any longer ignore.

A. M. JOOSTEN

Publisher's Note

In *From Childhood to Adolescence,* Maria Montessori applies her genius to the educational concerns of the older child—the adolescent and even the mature university student. At each level she looks at matters not from the point of view of the teacher seeking ways and means of transmitting the cultural heritage to the next generation, but rather from that of a clear-eyed scientist concerned with the unfolding and growth of that complex organism we call man. For each stage she seeks ways to facilitate optimum development.

As early as 1910, only three years after the first *casa dei bambini* opened its doors to very young slum children in Rome, Montessori turned her attention to education at higher levels. It was in Holland that the government endorsed Montessori methods at all educational levels and that a system of Montessori schools from pre-school through lyceum (high school) came into existence. In 1922 the Dutch government recognized Montessori primary schools; during World War II it permitted the Montessori lycea to hold their own final examinations, permitting those successful to enter the universities. The Municipal University of Amsterdam appointed Dr. Maria Montessori a lector in higher education.

Broadly grouping developmental levels, as does Piaget, Montessori first discusses the characteristics and needs of children from seven to twelve, showing that when a special environment is provided, the preadolescent is able and eager to apply himself to fields of study that have usually been reserved for the high school years. She finds that his interest in the world about him naturally leads him to inquire into the earth sciences and into experimentation and study in such areas as organic and inorganic chemistry. As examples, she presents several chapters dealing with subject matter that might be appropriate at this level. Her approach is similar to that of Jerome Bruner's spiral curriculum. On presenting a new concept, she says: "This idea remains indefinite in the imagination of the child but it corresponds to reality. Given that each of the details is later studied, it causes him to remember this view of the whole. So the knowledge, carrying its conclusions, radiates as though from a center, much as a seed develops little by little."

Montessori's ideas for the education of adolescents are as startlingly new today as her *casa dei bambini* was in 1907. She puts forth an "experimental school of social life," a school utterly different from our secondary schools. Her criticism of accepted practice is devastating: "The secondary school, such as it is at present, has no other aim than to prepare the pupils for a career, as if the social conditions of our lives were still peaceful and stable. . . . Not only does it not correspond to the social conditions of our day, but it is utterly bankrupt before the task it will have to take on: to protect and encourage the blossoming of the personalities of adolescents, the human energy on which the future depends." Today, decades later, it is only in the one area of health that we have solved problems that concerned Montessori. No longer do we see adolescence as a period when health is precarious, no longer does the specter of tuberculosis loom before us.

Montessori sees adolescence as the "sensitive period" for social relationships, the age at which the child must make a place for himself with his peers and at which he begins to consider the social realities of the wider community. Her experimental school for social life would be in a rural setting, where children and their predominantly young teachers would live in a self-contained community, self-governing and to a considerable extent self-supporting. Raising their own foodstuffs and perhaps running a guest house or store, they would learn about the work of the world at first hand.

Preparation for university entrance examinations would be provided for those students who wished to continue their education; it would coincide with the end of adolescence, when motivation for academic subjects is at its highest, much as it does at A. S. Neill's Summerhill School. Montessori believed that many universities of her day were merely diploma-granting institutions providing little more than an entry ticket into the professions and ignoring their true function: to prepare young adults, who are treated as adults, for a lifetime of research and inquiry.

Like much of Dr. Montessori's published work, this book bears the earmarks of her dynamic personality. She was an extraordinarily gifted and dramatic lecturer, and, although she knew several languages, she lectured in Italian and had a translator share the platform. It was often the transcriptions of these lectures, with little or no editing, that were turned into books.

The present book shows evidence that it was conceived as a series of lectures. These were assembled and translated into French, and first published in 1948. This English edition, translated from the French, makes *From Childhood to Adolescence* available to the English-speaking world for the first time. In it, Maria Montessori clearly speaks to the problems of our time, giving us new insights into what some of the unrest and dissatisfaction in our schools and colleges is all about.

MY VISION OF THE FUTURE is no longer of people taking exams and proceeding on that certification from the secondary school to the university, but of individuals passing from one stage of independence to a higher, by means of their own activity, through their own effort of will, which constitutes the inner evolution of the individual.

—MARIA MONTESSORI

1

The Successive Levels of Education

The Successive Levels
of Education

SUCCESSIVE levels of education must correspond to the successive personalities of the child.

Our methods are oriented not to any pre-established principles but rather to the inherent characteristics of the different ages. It follows that these characteristics themselves mark several levels.

The changes from one level to the other at these different ages could be compared to the metamorphoses of insects. When an insect comes out of the egg, it is very small and has a particular form and coloring. Then, little by little, it is transformed even though it remains an animal of the same species having the same needs and habits. It is an individual that *evolves*. Then one day something new happens. The insect spins his cocoon and becomes a chrysalis. The chrysalis in turn undergoes another slow evolution. Finally the insect comes out of the cocoon in the form of a butterfly.

We can establish a parallel between the life of the insect and that of the child. But the changing traits are not so clearly defined in the child as in the insect. It would be more exact to speak rather of "rebirths" of the child. In effect, we have before us at each new stage a different child who presents characteristics different from those he exhibited during preceding years.

1. Our first level of education, then, applies to the small child from birth to about seven years of age. Since a number of transfor-

mations take place during this important period, we have established the following subdivisions:

a) the first two years;
b) the years from three to five;
c) the sixth and seventh years.

2. For the period from seven to twelve years—the period immediately preceding adolescence—which may also be subdivided, we provide a different plan of education than for the preceding period. If the changes produced during the first period are considered as growth, it may be said that veritable metamorphoses take place during this one.

3. Twelve to eighteen years: one could say as much for this, the period of adolescence.

In each period we rediscover a growing being, but one who is a quite different person every time.

The last two levels will be considered consecutively. The first level has already been discussed in *The Discovery of the Child* and in *The Secret of Childhood*.

Only a thorough analysis leads to the discovery of the changes that occur continuously in the child, who grows until he becomes a man. It is precisely these changes that have the greatest bearing on the method of education.

The principles that can be applied usefully to the first period are not the same as those that must be applied to the second. We thus come to the practical part of education.

Let us use an example: When the small child begins to feel a loose tooth, it is a sign that the first period of childhood is over. This event occurs without much fanfare within the family. When the tooth becomes very loose it is pulled. A certain amount of fuss is made: the tooth is saved, and that little ceremony constitutes the first step of a new period in the life of the child. It will take a long time before all the baby teeth are gone and the child acquires his new teeth. But if, unluckily, it is necessary to pull one of the new teeth, more will be needed than merely a silk thread; we will have to deal with the extraction of a strong and fixed part. Loss of the baby teeth is only one among the many manifestations of this age.

All these traits—physical as much as psychic—constitute the links of the chain which is the metamorphosis of the child. He is both stronger and slimmer. His hair is less soft. Psychologically, he is less gentle, less accommodating.

2

Metamorphoses

Metamorphoses

FROM SEVEN to twelve years, the child needs to enlarge his field of action. As we have seen (in *The Secret of Childhood*), a limited environment is suited to the small child. There, social relations are established with others. In the second period the child needs wider boundaries for his social experiences. Development cannot result by leaving him in his former environment.

It is necessary that he come to understand, among other realities, what money ought to represent. Without money we could pass among the most marvelous things without ever being able to touch them. We would be like a bird with a broken beak dying of hunger on a pile of grain. Money is the means by which man procures things. That is why it attracts so much interest. We must consider money as the ''golden key'' that opens the door of supra–nature.''*

It is therefore necessary that children have first-hand experience in buying objects themselves and that they come to realize what they can buy with a unit of the money of their country.

What can one buy with one small coin? When I have used the coin to buy paper from the stationer, my coin has not disappeared. It will again buy more objects of its value. It is always the same

*Dr. Montessori thus calls the man-dominated and constructed human environment which man brings into being with the help of his own inner resources and those of nature—*trans*.

coin that passes from hand to hand, bringing the needed article to someone every time. How much merchandise can a coin minted fifty years ago have bought during those years? The money we handle is always the result of the work of men. It must always remain a means only.

The child needs, then, to establish social relationships in a larger society. The closed school, as it is conceived today, can no longer be sufficient for him. Something is lacking for the full development of his peronality. We note a certain regression —manifestations of his character which we call anomalies; they are merely his reactions to an environment that has become inadequate. But we do not notice that. And since it is understood that the child must do what adults tell him, even though his environment no longer suits his needs, if he does not comply we say that he is "naughty" and correct him. Most of the time we are unaware of the cause of his "naughtiness." Yet the child, by his conduct, proves what we have just said. The closed environment is felt as a constraint, and that is why he no longer wishes to go to school. He prefers to catch frogs or play in the street. These seemingly superficial factors prove that the child needs wider boundaries than heretofore.

"Render unto Caesar the things that are Caesar's, and to God the things that are God's." One part of our life belongs to God and the other part to man. It depends on him, on the surroundings of which we form a part, on our social life. When the child is placed in certain conditions that favor him, he manifests an extraordinary activity. His intelligence surprises us because all his powers work together as is normal for man. We are no longer dealing with the problem of transforming the methods of education: it is properly a problem of life that is being posed.

The spider's web occupies a much larger space than does the animal itself. The web represents the spider's field of action in acting as a trap for insects. It is constructed according to a plan. A thread secreted by the spider joins two branches, two rocks, two supports of any kind; then he weaves the rays. The construction proceeds according to a plan. Finally the spider weaves the thread around the center, going around at an always very carefully calculated distance. If the points of support are close together, the web is small. The greater the distance of one from the other, the larger the web will be. But it will always be woven with the same exactness according to a precise plan.

As is the web, so is the mind of the child constructed according to an exact plan. The abstract construction enables him to grasp what happens in his field, which was out of his range heretofore.

Depending on whether the child lives in a simple civilization or in a complicated world, his web will be more or less large and will enable him to attain more or fewer objectives.

This is why we must respect the interior construction and its manifestations, which may at times seem useless to us. The construction is necessary. It is thanks to this work that the child enlarges his psychic field and subsequently his receptive powers.

To consider the school as the place where instruction is given is one point of view. But to consider the school as a preparation for life is another. In the latter case the school must satisfy all the needs of life.

An education that suppresses the true nature of the child is an education that leads to the development of anomalies.

Scouting, which, outside of school, has brought an organized form of life to children, has therefore always interested us.

The passage to the second level of education is the passage from the sensorial, material level to the abstract. The need for abstraction and intellectual activity makes itself felt around the seventh year. Until that age the establishment of the relationships between objects is what is important to the child. This is to say that the child needs to classify and absorb the exterior world by means of his senses.

A turning toward the intellectual and moral sides of life occurs at the age of seven.

One could draw a parallel between the two periods. But they still remain on different levels. It is at seven years that one may note the beginning of an orientation toward moral questions, toward the judgment of acts. One of the most curious characteristics to be observed is the interest that occurs in the child when he begins to perceive things which he previously failed to notice. Thus he begins to worry about whether what he has done has been done well or poorly. The great problem of Good and Evil now confronts him. This preoccupation belongs to a very special interior sensitivity, the conscience. And this sensitivity is a very natural characteristic.

The seven-to-twelve-year-old period, then, constitutes one of particular importance for moral education. The adult must be aware of the evolution that is occurring in the mind of the child at this time and adapt his methods to conform with it.

If during the first period of development the teacher has used a very gentle approach and has intervened as little as possible in the activity of the child (activity which was above all motor and sensorial), it is to the moral level that his delicacy of approach ought now to be oriented. That is where the problem of this age lies. To think that the problem of morality only occurs later is to overlook the change that is already going on. Later, the moral problem becomes a good deal more difficult unless the child has been helped during this sensitive period. Social adaptations will become more thorny. It is at this age also that the concept of justice is born, simultaneously with the understanding of the relationship between one's acts and the needs of others. The sense of justice, so often missing in man, is found during the development of the young child. It is the failure to recognize this fact that engenders a false idea of justice.

The justice usually found around the school and in the family could be called "distributive justice"—that is to say, equality for all, as much in the distribution of punishments as of rewards. Special treatment of one individual seems to constitute an injustice; this introduces the concept of legal right. There is here an affirmation of individuality in the sense of egoism and isolation. Such a concept does not encourage interior development. On the other hand, justice—although usually not considered in this light—is born specifically from interior education. The principle of distributive justice and individual right, purely external, destroys the inborn, natural sense of true justice.

3

The Moral Characteristics of the Child from Seven to Twelve Years

The Moral Characteristics
of the Child from
Seven to Twelve Years

THE THREE characteristics we have just isolated for examination
—the child's felt need to escape the closed environment, the
passage of his mind to the abstract, and the birth in him of a moral
sense—serve as the basis for a scheme of the second period.

Once the child has gone beyond the limited area of the first
period, it is necessary for us to provide him with culture and to
enlarge his social experiences. Let us cite some important points
and note, in passing, the parallel that exists between this new
period and certain aspects of the preceding one.

Actually, the first period saw the child engaged in activities
which we have called "exercises of practical life." They constituted an effort to stretch the limits of the activities we considered
possible for him at that age. In this way the child, who has himself
stretched these limits, has won his independence. This is what
makes these exercises of patience, of exactness, and of repetition
so all-important.

The continuation of these exercises would be useless now that
the child is independent; that is to say, he knows how to devote
himself to an activity for which he will no longer need to ask help
of the adult, and he has coordination of movement. But the acts of
courtesy which he has been taught with a view to his making
contacts with others must now be brought to a new level. The
question of aid to the weak, to the aged, to the sick, for example,

now arises. This is not a question of training his movements: we begin the introduction of moral relationships, of those that awaken the conscience. If, up to the present, it was important not to bump someone in passing, it is now considerably more important not to offend that person.

If scouting has met with such success, it is because it has brought moral content to a group of children. It puts the accent on that which one ought or ought not to do. The children who belong to these groups generally do not do what scouting prohibits. In conforming to the rules of scouting, a new point of departure becomes attractive, a new dignity is born in the child.

Physical exercise, such as long hikes, also forms a part of the activities of these groups. The children become accustomed to the greater challenges of a more serious and a harder form of life.

While the younger child seeks comforts, the older child is now eager to encounter challenges. But these challenges must have an aim. The difference between a schoolteacher who takes children on a hike and an organization of this nature may be noted here. It is true that the former makes the children come out of the closed environment of the school and causes them to use their feet in walking and to see sensorially that which surrounds them. But this in no way increases the dignity of the child, who is still kept in a restricted circle. One may well multiply the number of hikes without changing anything, because the child's acceptance is passive. On the other hand, if the children consciously leave the school having a definite and freely chosen aim in mind, it is quite a different matter.

Now, scouting involves children who have applied voluntarily for membership in the society. And that society emphasizes, above all, a moral aim such as, for example, to protect the weak and to maintain a certain moral level; here the child may make commitments or not. No teacher obliges him to enter into the society; but if he wishes to be a member he must freely choose to obey its principles if he wishes to take part. The fact that he finds himself thus united with other individuals who have freely accepted the principles of a society constitutes the attraction of that society. Its limits are no longer the walls of a room but only the restraints of a moral order.

The scouts accept a regimen the rigors of which go far beyond what are considered possible for children of this age. Thus the long hikes, the nights in the open air, the responsibility for one's own actions, the fire, the camps, et cetera, all represent collective efforts. The basic moral principle requires a commitment from the individual: the commitment of the individual to the group. And that is what is essential.

As in the first period: We seek the child's consent to receive a lesson given. The lesson is now abstract when earlier it was sensorial.

In the second period there exist, then, possibilities superior to those we used to know in the child. Only, these possibilities are subordinate not to the command of someone, but rather to the command of the child's own conscience.

4

*The Needs of the Child
from Seven to Twelve Years*

The Needs of the Child
from Seven to Twelve Years

WHAT IS the practical approach to the education of a seven-year-old? First of all, let us always keep in mind the scheme we have outlined, which ought to give us an understanding of the child and enable us to help him in the attainment of his wishes—wishes he does not express but which we have guessed. It is this understanding that ought to be present from the start. We must sympathize with the little boy or girl who has changed, as much in his physical aspect (manner of dress, of combing his hair, et cetera) as in his inner person. He has become a strong being, a being who is entering into a new world, the world of the abstract. It is a rich world in which the acts accomplished by men will interest him more than the things. He has reached a new level, he starts to express judgements. This is new for him. Before, he was interested in things (changing the water for flowers, caring for the little fish, et cetera). Now he is interested mainly in the how and the why. All that used to attract him sensorially now interests him from a different point of view. He is looking for what needs to be done. That is, he is beginning to become aware of the problem of cause and effect.

But the adult finds this being, newly born to the world, a bit annoying. Therefore, without a new pedagogic directive, a new battle between the adult and this new child arises. The adult tires and responds by answering the abundance of questions either by begging the child to keep quiet or by giving excessively long explanations. He behaves as he did with the smaller child at the time he began to move: he bids him to keep still. Or he permits him, without judging properly, to become overexcited and to do everything he wants. The same misunderstanding takes place on the abstract plane: at each of his new births, the child must confront a new battle; at each of his new activities, however valuable, a new form of misunderstanding makes him suffer. It is, however, precisely up to the adult to assist the child's development by creating an environment adapted to his new needs. Just as it is necessary to help the baby while he is taking his first steps, so is it also necessary to help the child while he is taking his first steps in the world of abstraction.

Education ought to be a guide in this more critical period of life and of school. The teacher must again be made aware of his limitations, as we have already established with regard to the teacher of the smaller child. For the small child, he had to "count his words." Here he must be sure of what he ought to do, of what he ought to say, and of the extent to which he must reply to questions. He must be clearly conscious that his duty is to say little; to say only what is true, but not the whole truth in all its details. He must now also say what is "necessary and sufficient." It is indispensable to the child to feel the security the adult can and must give.

It is essential for the child, in all periods of his life, to have the possibility of activities carried out by himself in order to preserve the equilibrium between acting and thinking. His thoughts could, in effect, have the tendency to lose themselves in abstraction by reasonings without end just as the small child loses himself in a world of fantasy. We bring specific objects to the small child in an environment prepared for him. Here he acquires independence thanks to his own effort. And his activity gives him dignity. It is his own experience that brings him exact answers.

The role of education is to interest the child profoundly in an external activity to which he will give all his potential. We are concerned here with bringing him liberty and independence while interesting him in an activity through which he will subsequently discover reality. And for him this is the means by which he may free himself from the adult.

Let us examine the principal needs of the seven-year-old child. Something has changed in the body of this child. We see the difference at first glance in the teeth and the hair. Let us teach him dental hygiene and care of the hair. Then the feet and legs: the child of seven years has strong legs and seeks to escape from the closed circle. Instead of hemming him in, let us facilitate his mobility. In times gone by, man used to walk long distances. The hospitality offered the pilgrim used to consist first of all in the care of his feet, even before the offer of food. Let us give our imaginations free reign on the subject of these fundamentals of the history of humanity. Gabriel d'Annunzio used these symbolic words: "I kiss your feet that walk . . ."

Therefore, when the child shows us his desire to escape from the house, let us attract his attention somewhat solemnly to his feet. Thus, before setting out, he will be more conscious of what he is about to do. In attracting his attention to this part of his body, which may cause him to make a mistake, we lead him to think of the need to care for it, in order to walk, as much symbolically as practically.* It is on a higher plane that all these activities ought to be envisaged, which is to say, we will now educate the child on the abstract plane.

The foot is noble. To walk is noble. Thanks to the feet, the child who already walks can expect of the outdoors certain answers to his secret questions.

But it is necessary to prepare oneself to go out. The child in flight opens the door and goes. In teaching him the necessity of preparation, we oblige him to reflect. He understands that "to go out" consists of an activity that requires first the acquisition of information and materials.

The use of these things causes a series of practical exercises to come to mind. While for the very young the care of the wardrobe

---

*Similarly, many modern schools teach rules of bicycle safety and maintenance—*trans*.

remains purely esthetic, for the seven-year-old, clothes take on an importance in direct relation to his goal.

The first thing to do is to simplify the outing. It is necessary, then, to carry as few things as possible and, consequently, ''to choose.'' These material concerns eliminate the idea of flight. But since the instinct which urges flight exists, it is this instinct itself that excites a very active interest in the preparations. Step by step the response arises and the reasoning functions from cause to effect.

Let the teacher not lose sight of the fact that the goal sought is not the immediate one—not the hike—but rather to make the spiritual being which she is educating capable of finding his way by himself.

To understand the importance of these exercises, which ought to permit social experiences, we must not be content to consider the children's outing a simple health-giving exercise. It is designed to bring the child's attainments to life for him. It is only thus that their realities will penetrate him. That is what we call experience.

A child enclosed within limits however vast remains incapable of realizing his full value and will not succeed in adapting himself to the outer world. For him to progress rapidly, his practical and social lives must be intimately blended with his cultural environment. A general objection may be made that the child's schedule is already too crowded to introduce activities of a practical nature. This is an error, because it is a great deal more tiring to employ only half the faculties nature has bestowed on us. It is as though one were to walk on only one foot on the pretext that using both would be twice the work. Knowledge and social experience must be acquired at one and the same time.

The outing whose aim is neither purely that of personal hygiene nor that of a practical order, but that which makes an experience live, will make the child conscious of realities. It is up to the teacher to see to it that the moral teachings of life emerge from social experiences.

Morals have at the same time a practical side, which governs social relations, and a spiritual side, which presides over the awakening of conscience in the individual.

It is difficult to make social relations real if one uses only the imagination; practical experience is necessary. One cannot awaken the conscience by talking about it. The child must exercise a constant watch over his own activities. Thus education can resolve its problems while realizing itself when it seeks to resolve them by means of acts.

As walking entails the use of more than just the feet, it is necessary to assist one's step, to render it agile and able to function in all that forms part of the art. Let us not forget that these purposeful efforts will affect one's knowledge of the world.

Thus, when we are climbing, if all we think about is putting one foot before the other, fatigue will overtake us long before we reach our goal. But if we walk in a group, happy at the thought of the marvelous view we will surely discover up there, we will reach the summit without fatigue and will benefit in both joy and health. We have been morally conscious of our effort.

This act of consciousness does not cause any additional fatigue. Bring the child to the consciousness of his own dignity and he will feel free. His work will no longer weigh him down.

In the Netherlands five-year-old children ride bicycles on the streets. Swimming ought also to be taught. When one begins to leave the house it becomes necessary to think of one's personal defense. One has to prepare oneself, arm oneself, and acquire new skills. It is also necessary to learn to take care of one's clothes, to see that all is in order, to learn to sew on buttons, to remove spots, et cetera. We have prepared material to that end consisting of various textiles such as wool, silk, linen, cotton, et cetera, which we have soiled in different ways. The children are very interested in this exercise. The older children will not only learn to do all these things but they will also get the idea that before going out they ought to see that all their attire is in perfect order.

An individual who is not accustomed to allowing a spot to remain on his clothes will clean them immediately should they become soiled. He possesses a special sensitivity, an active sensibility which had to be developed. A child educated in this way knows how to recognize persons having this sensitivity. This causes him to develop the sense of caring about the correctness of his own person and constant self-inspection. He does not wish to have any trace of disorder on his person, nor does he wish to leave any trace of disorder in his wake.

Another useful exercise is to wrap packages. In order to make a nice package one must first of all take measurements and work methodically. One also needs to know how to prepare and pack what is required for a meal outdoors (plates, glasses, utensils, et cetera).

It is also very important for the child who goes out to know how to orient himself in the field, to recognize the position of the sun, the cardinal compass points, how to guess the approximate time of day, et cetera. We have him observe, for example, that moss is found mainly on the north side of trees in a forest. We have him predict the weather from the clouds and study the direction of the wind. All these things arouse his attention and become actual knowledge. When the children begin to become interested in these things they talk about them to their juniors, thereby handing down their own riches. In this way, when the older ones go out they carry with them knowledge and civilization, which is to say, progress. And a superior atmosphere is created around them.

All these activities constitute a symbol of life. Since life outdoors differs from life in a closed environment, a guide and an aim are necessary. In short, to go out, one must be ready for it.

If we would have the same concept for the second period as for the first, we would need to let the child go, to go where he would. At first he will get lost.

Previously, the perfect teacher was one who allowed the child to act, effacing herself. This procedure is not applicable now. The second-period child is living two parallel existences, his home existence and his existence in society. This is new. The scouts offer some useful elements here. When they go hiking they do exercises conducive to agility. Practical experience is also useful at this age. These children, when biking, observe the objects left for a purpose by those who preceded them; these signs along the route help them to find their way. Also, the groups who follow separately learn to recognize, by the position of a given object considered as a signal, the direction they themselves must take. This is an active exercise that habituates the children to observe, to seek. This method is altogether different from that which consists of walking with a child while holding him by the hand.

Another scout activity is that of studying animal tracks. We made the very small children notice the smallest details of the environment. It was in this way that they learned to move dexterously, to touch objects without causing them to fall, without breaking them, et cetera. Likewise, now the more evolved child develops by observing all in his universe. The choice of exercises is a function of his age. There are considerations of a physical nature which must take first place in making the choice. The exercises pertaining to movement are dictated more by the age of the child than by the level of his intelligence.

An example: A young child in a school in the Netherlands knew how to do the square of the binomial. This would compare to the knowledge of children much older. But one day, having asked his teacher whether he could collect spent matches in the forest with his playmates, he did not behave differently from the other children. Like them, he was only occupied with knowing who would find the most, without thinking about the explanations being given by his teacher elsewhere. This concern gave his age away. A small child still interests himself in little things even though his intelligence is capable of bounding toward much more advanced concepts. One could say that even though a child can escape on the intellectual plane, on the practical plane he remains tied to his age.

5

The Passage to Abstraction—
The Role of the Imagination,
or "Going Out," the Key to Culture

The Passage to Abstraction—
The Role of the Imagination
or "Going Out," the Key to Culture

WHEN ONE thinks about preparing children to go out of the closed environment where they have been educated up to the age of seven years, a vast panorama comes to mind. To go out of a classroom to enter the outside world, which includes everything, is obviously to open an immense door to instruction. The event is comparable to the appearance of Comenius' *Orbis Sensualium Pictus* in the history of pedagogy.

Before Comenius, scanty knowledge was passed on by the exclusive use of words. Comenius conceived of offering the universe to children by means of pictures—and it seems that it was the initial building block of a new method of education. The amount of knowledge must have increased greatly because of this.

He assembled a book of pictures representing everything that makes up the world: plants, animals, rocks, peoples, geographic maps, historic facts, industry, commerce, medicine, sanitation, a reproduction of the first machines, the way in which they functioned, et cetera, each idea being represented by an image and a brief commentary in words. It seemed easy for the mind to embrace everything looking at the images in the book. It was really a first example of what later became an encyclopedia, except that the encyclopedia returned to the use of the word while *Orbis Sensualium Pictus* remains just about unique in the history of pedagogy.

And yet the idea has remained. A beginning was made to teach by using tangible objects adapted for handling. But just as ideas lose strength in becoming widespread, the method of Comenius —who knew everything—was weakened by the teacher who presented only her meager knowledge put into pictures.

Later, it was thought that representation in only two dimensions is insufficient for the child's comprehension. Then he was offered objects of knowledge in their natural form. But to overcome the difficulty of procuring and preserving objects, they were placed in museums. Every self-respecting modern school must have a museum. In this way enclosed objects may be found near confined children. The adult, underestimating the intelligence of the child, surrounds him with a depressing atmosphere, while what he needs is to *see* things in order to understand them. The capacity of childhood intelligence remains unsuspected. What we hope—we to whom the child has revealed the power of his intelligence—is to revise the idea of Comenius by bringing the world itself to the children.

When the child goes out, it is the world itself that offers itself to him. Let us take the child out to show him real things instead of making objects which represent ideas and closing them in cupboards.

In its entirety, the world always repeats more or less the same elements. If we study, for example, the life of plants or insects in nature, we more or less get the idea of the life of all plants or insects in the world. There is no one person who knows all the plants; it is enough to see one pine to be able to imagine how all the other pines live. When we have become familiarized with the characteristics of the life of the insects we see in the fields, we are able to form an idea of the life of all other insects. There has never been anyone who has had all the insects of the universe available to his view. The world is acquired psychologically by means of the imagination. Reality is studied in detail, then the whole is imagined. The detail is able to grow in the imagination, and so total knowledge is attained. The act of studying things is, in a way, meditation on detail. This is to say that the qualities of a fragment of nature are deeply impressed upon an individual.

After seeing a river or a lake, is it necessary to see all the rivers and lakes of the world to know what they are? The imagination, afterward, is able to form a concept of the world. A machine, a man who fishes, a man who works—these are all details that go to form knowledge. This is a universal means of organizing culture. It is self-evident that the possession of and contact with real things bring with them, above all, a real quantity of knowledge. The inspiration engendered by it revitalizes the intelligence that was interested and wished to know. From all these things new intellectual interests arise (climates, winds, et cetera). Instruction becomes a living thing. Instead of being illustrated, it is brought to life. In a word, the outing is a new key for the intensification of instruction ordinarily given in the school.

There is no description, no image in any book that is capable of replacing the sight of real trees, and all the life to be found around them, in a real forest. Something emanates from those trees which speaks to the soul, something no book, no museum is capable of giving. The wood reveals that it is not only the trees that exist, but a whole, inter-related collection of lives. And this earth, this climate, this cosmic power are necessary for the development of all these lives. The myriads of lives around the trees, the majesty, the variety are things one must hunt for, and which no one can bring into the school.

How often is the soul of man—especially that of the child —deprived because one does not put him in contact with nature. And when this contact is considered, it is only for reasons of health. How could a child describe the difference in nature as seen in daylight and as seen at night when, in our time, he must inexorably go to bed in the evening?

I heard a comment from the mouth of an eight-year-old child which profoundly impressed me: "I would give anything to be able, one night, to see the stars." He had heard them being discussed but he had never seen them. His parents thought it necessary not to allow the child to stay up a single evening on any pretext whatever. All that hygiene, centered on the physical person, has made the world neurotic. It is noted that mental health has diminished in spite of the progress which improves physical health. If tension among adults has increased abnormally, it is because they have formed an erroneous idea of life. These prejudices create as many obstacles in the intellectual life of the child. What harm would come from allowing a child to rise later if, as an exception, he were to be allowed to satisfy the interest he takes in discovering the stars or the sounds of the night? The mind of the child is found to be at this age on an abstract level. He is not satisfied with a mere collection of facts; he tries to discover their causes. It is necessary to make use of this psychological state, which permits the viewing of the things in their entirety, and to let him note that everything in the universe is interrelated. Thus when the child wants to understand the causes of a whole complex of effects, the world, which he has before him, can fill that normal need.

But it is not always as easy to present the whole as it is to present a detail. Then it does not suffice for the teacher to limit herself to loving and understanding the child. She must first love and understand the universe. She must therefore prepare herself and work at it. Certainly the child is still central. But the teacher must now appeal to that part of the child which finds itself in the world of the abstract. When the child was very small it was enough to call him by name for him to turn around. Now we must appeal to his soul. To speak to him is not enough for this; it is necessary to interest him. What he learns must be interesting, must be fascinating. We must give him grandeur. To begin with, let us present him with the world.

In Genesis it says: "God created the heavens and the earth." It is a very simple statement but it has grandeur, and the mind stays awake. When details are presented as being parts of a whole, they become interesting. The interest increases in proportion to the gain in knowledge. In addition, the knowledge presented now must not be on the same scale as before. It must not be purely sensorial anymore. Now the child must have constant recourse to his imagination. Imagination is the great power of this age. Since we are unable to present everything, it is up to the child to use his imagination. The .instruction of children from seven to twelve years of age must appeal to the imagination. A configuration of reality must spring from the imagination. It is necessary therefore to be strictly precise. Exactness, as a numeral and as all that makes up mathematics, will serve to build that configuration of reality. Now what is it that strikes the imagination? Above all, grandeur and, next, mystery. The imagination is then able to reconstruct the whole when it knows the real detail.

Imagination was not given man for the simple pleasure of fantasizing any more than were the four characteristics common to man (language, religion, death rites, and arts) given to let him live on contemplation. Imagination does not become great until man, given the courage and strength, uses it to create. If this does not occur, the imagination addresses itself only to a spirit wandering in emptiness.

Obstacles abound in the world. But man's spiritual life gives him the strength to surmount them to accomplish his task. Love of the homeland is based on imagination. Is it not that which gives us the idea of what our country is and who our compatriots are? Our fight on behalf of children also needs imagination, because we ourselves know only very few children.

The homeland, and those children we thus imagine, do indeed exist and we know it.

He who does not possess the world of the imagination is poor. But the child with too much fantasy is a disturbed child. We do not know how to calm him. We do not say: "Let us suppress the imagination of that child's mind," but rather: "*The child's imagination is insufficient for his mind.*" We must nourish the other facet of his intelligence, that which has to do with the external world and his activity. It is in this way that we will help him grow in discipline.

The child's imagination is vague, imprecise, without limits. But from the moment he finds himself in contact with the external world *he requires precision*. This requirement is such that the adult would be unable to impose it. Its full potential lies within the child. When a child's interest is aroused on the basis of reality, the desire to know more on the subject is born at the same time. At such a moment exact definitions may be presented. Children express the desire for such definitions in their own way. For example, in one of our schools there was once a seven-year-old boy who chose to study the Rhine. The teacher had prepared a map of the river and its tributaries, but the child was not satisfied with it. He wanted to know the relative length of each of the tributaries. (Here we see the idea of mathematics awakened.) He used graph paper to draw a better map. It was in this way that the sense of proportional size and the interest in study were born in him at the same time. He remained at the same task, by his own choosing, for more than two months. He was not satisfied until he had meticulously completed it. His satisfaction came with his being able to express these concepts in mathematical terms.

Let us draw a parallel here with the smaller children who by touching objects trained their hands to ever greater lightness of touch. The exercise seemed to satisfy something inside of them. Touching for the younger child is what imagining is for the older one. On the former age level we would have worked on the sensorial plane as, for the latter, we work on the level of the imagination. Thus at different levels we encounter parallel phenomena. With the little children the response was infantile. But it is still true that knowledge may truly be developed by awakening the interest. A detail of physics or chemistry is enough to produce the awakening. At the same time, a number of experiments and conclusions arise which bring learning in depth and detail.

The mind bases itself on the imagination, which brings things to a higher level, that of abstraction. But the imagination has need of support. It needs to be built, organized. Only then may man attain a new level. He is penetrating the infinite.

A study outline here presents itself: *to bring the whole by means of the presentation of detail*. Thus, when we wish to consider the study of living beings, the most important thing is first to establish the classification. It has been an error to have sought to suppress it. It has seemed too dry and too difficult, even though it constitutes a precise key for the study of the whole. Not only does the classification help in understanding, but it also aids the memory. Therefore it constitutes a base which one should establish first of all.

Would that the teacher allowed herself to be imbued by the grandeur of this whole to be able to transmit it to the child. It is not only the classification of a few details that must be the point of departure, but the classification of the Whole. And this Whole, emerging at the same time, will serve as the base so that each detail comes to be located in the mind. For example, let us say that the world is this globe on whose surface we live. But let us say immediately that this planet receives reflections from the world of the stars. One cannot, then, isolate it from the whole; one cannot content oneself with observing it all alone. Considered in the abstract, we can envisage it as the empire of three kingdoms —animal, vegetable, and mineral. We show a globe, entirely different from the one used for geography. We only represent in brown what depicts the land, and in blue what depicts the water. This globe does not serve in the study of geography, but is intended to stimulate the imagination, which starts working around this kind of globe.

To speak of animals, of vegetables, of minerals is an abstraction. But we will say here: "Man lives in the world and man must conquer it." The intelligence of man must conquer the world as the intelligence of the little child has conquered the environment.

All is strictly interrelated on this planet. And one notes that each science studies only the details of a total knowledge. To speak afterward of the life of man on the surface of the globe is to speak of history. And each detail holds the child's interest by reason of its strict relation to the others. We may compare it with a tapestry: each detail is a piece of embroidery; the whole constitutes a magnificent cloth.

To give the child of seven to twelve years the idea of a whole in nature, for example of the planet on which we live, we must begin by bringing him numbers.

To do well, it is necessary to aim at giving an idea of all the sciences, not in precise detail but only as an impression. The idea is to "sow the seeds of the sciences" at this age, when a sort of sensitive period for the imagination exists. Once the idea has been presented, we must show that a science extends from each branch: mineralogy, biology, physics, chemistry, et cetera. And, as we have seen, the examination of a detail triggers the study of the whole.

It is understood that one is obliged to begin by the study of a detail. But since nothing exists that does not constitute a part of the whole, it is sufficient to choose any one detail which will then become a point of departure in the study of the whole.*

---

*Later Dr. Montessori prepared a slightly different globe for small children in the Children's House. On it the land portions were covered with real sand (glued on) and the water parts by smooth, blue enamel paint. This more sensorial globe thus added a tactile impression to the visual one (*cf.* the rough-smooth exercises with touch material)—*trans*.

6

Water

Water

TO BEGIN, it is necessary to choose an element that is large, even quantitatively, because if an element is present in large quantities its function must be important. Thus, water is one of the most imposing elements of the earth. Let us say at the outset that many animals live in the water, especially in the oceans, and that these animals themselves elicit a great deal of interest. And since imagination could never suffice to give an idea of the number of these animals, the decimal system, by means of which we may construct enormous numbers, comes to our aid. And mathematics in this way helps the imagination.

In order to form an idea of the quantities, one could say that certain fish deposit 70×10^4 eggs per year. And one could add that other very small animals exist in such great numbers that the largest number a child is capable of writing would not be sufficient. Show these little animals by means of the microscope and say that sometimes a group of them causes a large spot to form on the sea, a spot so large that it would take a ship six days to circumnavigate it. The mind is thus helped more precisely than by simply saying: "This quantity is very large, it is immense."

We have the children note that the beings which live on the land are found only on the surface, while those of which we have just spoken are found throughout the depth of the water; that the depth is often such as to be able to contain the highest mountains. This will help to give an idea of the relationship existing between the beings that live on land and those that live in the seas. The contrast is even greater when one considers that large deserts, almost uninhabited, are found on the land, while the water of the seas abounds in almost all its parts with animals.

What is it that maintains the state of sanitation in the world? If the water of the seas is analyzed, it is found always to be composed in the same manner. The composition may be determined exactly, mathematically. And for how long has the water been of this composition? Always. Why? If it should ever change, even to the minutest degree, all the living beings found there would die.

And there the vital problem of water has been broached.

SUBDIVISION OF THE STUDY OF WATER

Water is very interesting. We need to understand it. Like almost all bodies, it takes three physical states: solid, liquid, and gaseous. Let us emphasize this, because water presents itself to us under these three aspects more commonly than do other substances. Even in the solid state it takes various forms (snow, ice), it seems as if by whim. We are able to cause the three forms by means of heat (by cooling or heating it). Since these transformations are so easy to obtain, is it not logical that we use it as our measuring standard? Thus it serves to measure the temperature, and we say: "0° is the point at which water changes to ice. 100° is the point at which water changes to vapor. The interval between these two points is divided into 100 equal parts, thereby giving us centigrade degrees."

We can practically see water transform itself into vapor. Thus changed, it is much lighter than it was when cooler. It has this in common with the other substances. Only, for water, this is not exact except beginning from 4° above zero. In effect, under 4° it is lighter again. This is a property specific to water. And this is the reason that, in rocks where it has penetrated as a liquid, it increases in volume on cooling and causes them to split just as it causes the pipes of the plumbing to split. Such incidents occur continually in nature. Water therefore continues its work constantly.

This phenomenon is a blessing to the beings that live in water, because if it were heavy in the solid state it would crush them all upon solidifying. Instead, it becomes a veritable protection for them. Let us note that the laws of nature are not absolute. It is necessary that water become lighter upon solidifying, and this occurs contrary to all the laws. If water were an animal, one could say that it acts this way by adaptation. The phenomena of nature are always instructive when examined without prejudice.

When solid substances are introduced into water, only the water evaporates, leaving the solid substances behind. It is in this way that the water evaporated from the seas forms the clouds above the earth and falls again as rain. But the solids it contained are left in the sea. Clouds attract a great deal of interest; their magnificence arouses this interest. And what also excites the curiosity is water in the nonliquid state.

Let us broach the study of water in the liquid state by beginning with the problem of the rivers which carry solids in suspension to the sea. The water of the rivers is, in fact, abundantly charged with salts. Here again mathematics helps the imagination. To say that the rivers carry an enormous quantity of salts is all right. But to say the Mississippi alone discharges 70 million kilograms of limestone daily into the sea, and that all the other rivers do likewise in proportion, immediately causes questions like, "Where does all the limestone go? And since when has this been occurring? And how is it that the sea water is not saturated with all that salt? How has it been able to maintain the exact composition necessary for fish life to continue? What happens? Does the material disappear? Is it a miracle?" No. Something happens which permits the earth to continue to exist. And when we see ships sailing on the oceans let us bring our thoughts again to the water in which a continual work is being carried out to maintain its composition intact.*

*The principle of the cosmic theory was inspired by a book well known in Italy: *Acqua ed Aria* by the celebrated geologist Antonio Stoppani (1824-1891), an uncle of Maria Montessori's mother, Renilde Stoppani.

The idea has been launched. Everything is interrelated and, beginning with a detail, one arrives at the whole by correlation.

Water is also a solvent. Certain substances can be dissolved in it. When they are dissolved they disappear from view (for example, sugar).

The great cosmic function of water is to dissolve rock. It dissolves, in fact, immense masses, equal to mountains thousands of meters high, which we may have imagined to be the most durable materials on earth.

This part of the study of water—the most mysterious because it concerns what the eye does not see—is precisely the one that arouses the most interest. We explain, then, that the water dissolves the limestone contained in the rock. This curious function gives an idea of the immense quantity of limestone existing on the surface of the earth.

In order to realize how much limestone there is, we compare it to a prism with a base twice the size of Europe and 10,000 feet high. Such precise comparisons aid the imagination.

Let us see how the process occurs. The water seizes the limestone, absorbs it, and carries it away. If we do not see this take place it is because the water takes a long time to accomplish its task and we are accustomed to perceive only the work of a moment. But a number of experiences permits us to establish that the water does indeed act this way—the little holes or pockmarks which may be noted on ancient monuments and the paving stones in parks are similarly marked, et cetera. We shall return to this subject when we discuss the action of water on land.

Water, the great sculptor of rocks, carries substances by various means, including rivers. And if we wish to give an idea of the extent of rivers on the earth, there is no need to make the subject weighty. Let us glance at a map. There we will see that a single river—itself and its tributaries—covers a vast area of the earth. The children are impressed by the great rivers which collect water from all parts of the earth, and which bring it to the seas together with all the dissolved substances. We should give many presentations of these rivers. There is no need yet to name the tributaries, but the sight of them stimulates the imagination.

We now help the children to observe that all the great rivers of the earth spill water and salts into a single ocean, the Atlantic, either directly or by intermediaries in the form of other seas (Arctic Ocean, Mediterranean Sea, et cetera) which are in constant communication with it. And if some great rivers spill elsewhere, into the Pacific, for example, little islands form at their mouths, barriers intended to protect the Pacific Ocean. We may say, then, that the Atlantic is the collector of all such substances.

We have already mentioned the immense quantity of salts the Mississippi alone carries to the sea. All the other rivers function in a similar fashion. The water subsequently changes to vapor but abandons the substances which it was carrying. Destructive water, a gentle worker, so fresh, works tranquilly. A great quantity of calcareous (chalky) substances remains on deposit at the bottom of the sea. The reason the Atlantic has not been filled by now is that the substances have been distributed into all the other seas. This phenomenon of distribution constitutes another branch of study which may, in part, be included in physical geography (for example, the ocean currents). We will discuss them later.

What is truly impressive is that all the limestone carried to the sea during hundreds of thousands of years has in no way changed the composition of the water. The lives of all the beings that live in the sea depend on this constancy. The cosmic problem therefore consists in causing the evacuation of all that calcium carbonate in order that the water remain unchanged. But how may what is dissolved be eliminated? It is impossible to boil the water of the sea! It is here that another active force intervenes within the sea itself. It is an energy whose task is to fix all the dissolved substances. And this energy is Life. There exist, in fact, live animals that fix the calcium carbonate.

There exist, then, on the one hand, destructive physical forces, and, on the other, live reconstructed forces. From time immemorial there have been animals exercising this function. They are those who dress themselves in shells and who constitute a veritable force charged with the task of seizing the excessive calcium carbonate and fixing it.

The study of aquatic shells is very interesting to children. There are shells so big that a single one of their valves weighs 300 kilograms; there are tiny, microscopic ones—as, for example, the foraminifers—whose fragments may be shown to the children under the microscope since they are invisible to the naked eye. They are unicellular beings which form a type of dust comparable to that of the desert. The dust, on collecting, forms calcareous deposits.

The animals having the most important function in this domain are the corals, which have the important property of remaining stationary. While absorbing limestone they multiply and grow until they reach the surface to form islands, vast regions. Indicating on the one hand the existence of rivers on the earth and, on the other, the existence of coral formations, one may discover that these powers have a relation one to the other. One represents the forces that destroy, and the other the energies that simultaneously reconstruct.

The very quantity of the coral islands is an interesting point to bring to the children's attention. Continents are disappearing while others are being constructed. Today we know these islands well, and we may note that in the Pacific they form a continent comparable to Asia. What is curious is that all these constructions are situated in the Pacific Ocean and not in the Atlantic where, in fact, the rivers carry the materials. Let us see why.

It is known that the corals need calm and pure water in which to live. The storehouse of the materials required is in the Atlantic. And the beings that use the materials live very far away. This is similar to what occurs in industry (production takes place in one locality and, far away, the men in a quieter locality use the products). It is a marvelous organization that places the production or storehouse in one rather turbulent place and the consumption and reconstruction elsewhere. Who then transports the substances so far to the immobile corals? The means of communication must exist, as must the means of distribution of these important materials (precisely as for the distribution and transport of industrial products). So we begin to see the living organization, mysterious in itself, but simple to understand. We touch on *physical geography;* on *zoology,* to explain the function of life in the universe; on *mineralogy;* also on certain principles of *physics,* referring to the properties of water; and also on elements of *chemistry,* to explain how water is able to destroy rocks.

All these elements form parts of a whole, intensely interesting as a story. They will tell us the History of the Earth.

A classification of shells is often given. But there is such a variety of them with names so difficult that it seems impossible to consider the imposition of this study as sufficiently important to the children. Now, what must immediately be given the children is not the description of all the shells—univalves, bivalves, et cetera —but rather the idea of the immense variety of forms taken on by nature. What strikes the imagination is this, as well as the esthetic talents of the creatures, which do not merely cover themselves with shells for the sake of covering themselves but design those shells in various forms, adorn the designs in a great diversity of ways, each species being different from the others, just as man does not construct his house while thinking only of sheltering himself. Let us attract the child's attention to the work of life. That is what is important. If the animals were endowed with intelligence and were able to discern an aim in their work, doubtless they would think: "We work to maintain the purity of the oceans; and we exert considerable effort in order to carry away all the calcium carbonate which, without us, would provoke the death of all the seas' inhabitants." But they would not be able to imagine that they are builders of new lands, of new chains of mountains, and that it is they who form the islands on which new creatures will establish themselves. The real aim of living beings is, in fact, far removed from the apparent one. It would seem at first glance that their function is to seek the best, the happiest conditions of existence. Corals could then be thought to be seekers of a good time. It is indeed curious to see how they strive to live well, seeking a certain temperature, assuring themselves of water that contains much chlorine; they live in salubrious surroundings (as we do when we go to live in the country) far from the agitated and filthy things which are the rivers arriving from the land. It matters little to them that it is the rivers that bring the materials for their use. They try to be as far removed from them as possible in splendid locations, temperate and healthy. They wish to live hygienically. But their work—which is essential—consists in absorbing the water, appropriating the calcium carbonate, and returning purified water. All the beings that secrete have the same aim. The quantity of water absorbed by them is considerable. It equals, in proportion, the absorption by a man of thirty liters of water per second.

The corals do such a great work that they need help. To that end there are little algae which work constantly to furnish them with oxygen. One may compare the corals to the masters of servants. It would seem that we have to do with fantastic tales. And yet, all this is reality—but reality that ought to satisfy the imagination.

The corals remain stationary. Someone is needed to carry the requisite calcium carbonate to them. So we discover a vast communications organization (an important chapter which corresponds in human society to the means for commercial communications). We come, in this way, to marine and submarine currents. Let us look at them on the map. They are the means of communication between two oceans.

The movement of water, which is quite complicated, is dependent upon a large number of factors (many of which are cosmic). But the currents are not sufficient to create the movement necessary to deliver the calcium carbonate to the secreting animals. We must, therefore, consider also the movement of the animals. Interest brings us immediately to the higher animals, the fish which occur in infinite variety but whose general type may be described thus: two great masses of muscle which move, much as a spoon moves the sugar at the bottom of a cup, without ever stopping.

We may therefore examine two large groups of animals, the heavy secreters that reamain on the bottom of the sea without ever, or almost ever, moving, and the fish that move continually. The latter have a light skeleton which barely suffices to support the muscles of movement.

The infinite variety of fish forms a group having particular social relationships. Let us, then, study *the lives of fish in the seas*.

The life of fish is very interesting. And what is more interesting yet is their perpetual movement whose cosmic purpose is to move the water. And how pleasant this movement makes the life of the fish! ("Happy and free as a fish in water.") It is important to note that the fulfillment of a great work brings with it the happiness of the living beings who are charged with it. But one may hardly express this idea without the logic of it becoming obvious. To accomplish a great work it is necessary, in fact, to be situated in the best possible conditions.

It is difficult to study the various ocean currents. But it is easy to look at them traced on a chart. And we may tell the children that immense rivers exist not only on land but also in the oceans.

How is it possible to have water currents in water? For the sea is furrowed with currents. One could apply oneself to a sort of anatomical study of the ocean to know exactly the routes of such currents.

The water of the ocean also has its exact, eternal laws. One current always goes in the same direction while another current goes in another direction. And the study of these currents reveals the existence of those found at greater depths. There are exterior factors (such as the temperature, the sun, the attraction of the sun and the moon) and interior factors at the basis of the movement. Among the interior factors is the work of the animals to attract the water down from the surface and to cause it to rise again. One could also compare this circulation with that of blood in the body of an animal. The impure blood goes to the lungs where it is purified and returns pure. Likewise, the secreting animals of which we have spoken represent the lungs of the ocean. They purge the water of the calcium carbonate which it contains and they do this without ever stopping. The process is carried out on a large scale, as if the earth were a living person. This idea remains indefinite in the imagination of the child but it corresponds to reality. Given that each of the details is later studied, it causes him to remember this view of the whole. So the knowledge, carrying its conclusions, radiates as though from a center, much as a seed develops, little by little.

The study of streams on the surface brings us to *geography*. The streams, red on the map if warm, blue if cold, are easily located by the child. His imagination may be helped by our telling him that each of the currents is an enormous river carrying a quantity of water corresponding to a thousand Mississippi and Amazon Rivers combined. We follow, for example, the equatorial current from the Gulf of Mexico. When it separates, one of its branches forms the Gulf Stream and the other returns in part until it completes the loop. The movement of the currents may be compared to the exercises of practical life. As when one sweeps a room, all the sweepings are accumulated in one corner before being picked up, so here the calcium carbonate disappears. At the extremity of the loop a collector is in fact to be found, the Sargasso Sea.

Because the currents cause a circular movement, it may be noticed that objects along the circumference are thrown out on the tangent. The objects are thrown out by centrifugal force (for example, pieces of wood and even whole trees) and the routes taken by them are always the same. The hard work of the water always carries the flotage to the same places. This is why, even though no vegetation exists in the frozen regions, a quantity of pieces of wood may be found there. They are used by the inhabitants to build whole cities, and to provide heat for themselves. These anecdotes are as interesting to the children as fables.

Let us keep our eyes on the map an instant longer. It is necessary to expose things to children for sufficient time to attract their attention. Since they assimilate the environment by instinct, they assimilate at the same time that which we have put out. Each applies himself to the work that he has chosen. But the map remains in place. It interests the child. We note that the currents are all parallel in the Pacific, which is warm. Elsewhere, on the other hand, their courses are tortuous.

By visual observation of the currents it may be concluded that cold water is denser and sinks, while warm water, being lighter, rises. Also, the water purified of calcium is lighter than that which has not yet been purified and it rises to the surface.

The anecdote of the bottle containing a note, thrown into the sea by a shipwrecked person at the tip of Cape Horn and found in Ireland, is a proof of the movement of water.

Certainly one would like to be able to penetrate the mysteries and the majesty inherent in water. In this way the desire to celebrate it in verse is also born. Its mode of action, its intelligent aim, its grandiose mission cause its maternity to be suspected. Is it not, in fact, the mother of all these living beings, the agents of Creation? Saint Francis of Assisi understood this well for, in an outburst of fraternal love for the elements, he sang the praises of "Sister Water who is very useful and humble and precious." It is loved by all because all living beings—plants and animals—are thirsty and cannot live without it. Why would we not admire it and feel gratitude for it as well as the desire to know more about it? The study of water, then, can become a passion, and the precise conclusions reached by a direct knowledge of it elucidate such a study.

We now look at water from a different point of view. We have already spoken to the child of its property as a solvent and we have seen that its great cosmic function is to dissolve rock. We therefore consider water to be a dissolver. That is already something precise. We now consider the mechanism of this property, which brings us quite naturally to *chemistry*.

We say that water, in its quality as a "solvent," becomes a "solution." We show that its power to dissolve has very well-defined limits which may be measured. Here the mathematical factor again comes into play. We describe the water that remains at the surface as being "saturated," and we indicate that the surplus forms a "deposit." We then mix another well-known substance, starch, into the water and show that, even in small quantities, starch is not soluble. It mixes but it never dissolves. We then say that the starch remains "in suspension," and we have just used another precise term. Following this, we put a pebble into water to see that it does not dissolve.

Water is nevertheless an excellent solvent. While it is true that there are certain substances it cannot dissolve, it is curious that those it does dissolve are harbored passively. Now, its greatest craving is for rock and it has never ceased to devour it. It travels to the depths of the earth in its search. Then why is it that the pebble we put into water did not dissolve? Whatever may the mystery be? Something a little different requiring a complementary explanation must be lurking here. Not only does water dissolve solid substances but it also dissolves certain gases, in particular carbon dioxide. This gas is expelled by all animals and the earth itself emits it continually. Water, before it can act on rock, must be charged with this gas which is therefore also found to subsist in the ocean.

Since the water is unable, alone, to carry rocks away, it first transforms it by means of this gas. What we wish to say is that the rock is first made friable, then it is carried away by the water.

These transformations are different from those that one obtains by means of a simple solution. Water, as is learned in chemistry, works on the rock by an action that is both physical and chemical at the same time.

Let us then show a bottle of water that can contain a large quantity of carbon dioxide under pressure—in other words, a supersaturated solution of carbonic acid. Water that penetrates the earth may also contain a large quantity of this gas precisely because it is under pressure. This is what happens when it digs underground galleries and wells. But when the water comes out of the earth it restores all the surplus of calcium carbonate which it possessed under pressure. It is at this time that it produces the large mineral formations on the surface of the earth. Tufa and travertine are two examples of this. The action is comparable to that which occurs when a bottle under pressure allows carbon dioxide to escape and the pressure to fall when it is opened.

The water therefore has gone underground where it has charged itself with rock, which it carries to the surface and deposits. The rock, like a veritable mason, will form constructions.

Water is active, has a hearty appetite, and is capable of containing an enormous quantity of this gas for which it is avid and which is its collaborator in the important work of devouring the rock. This is why, during heavy rains, the water, which falls more charged with carbon dioxide than it was as a vapor, leaves its traces on the rock.

7

Some Chemistry Experiences

Some Chemistry Experiences

FROM OUR examination of the currents on the maps we have given the child the idea that some liquids are heavier than others and that the lighter liquids lie over the heavier ones. Let us now offer some greater precision obtained by means of exercises that will teach the technical and scientific terms, even some having no connection with those used for the currents. These exercises are parallel to those of practical life which helped the smaller children in learning to make precise movements. Thus, the use of test tubes and funnels constitutes a new manual exercise for the new stage. Certain actions are comparable to those the child performed when he poured water into a glass. But here even more attention is required because the container is smaller.

Let us, then, pour liquids of different weights into a test tube—the term ''specific weight'' is introduced. The best way to understand this term is to see the strata of the different liquids: at the bottom we have mercury; we pour water in next, then oil, and finally methyl alcohol. In order to identify them better, we color each of the liquids differently.

Figure 1.

Then we take two test tubes, putting water and crystallized sugar in one, water and starch in the other.

The sugar crystals dissolve slowly, so that we could doubt their solubility in water. But if we apply heat, the sugar soon disappears. In place of a *cold solution* we obtain a *warm solution*.

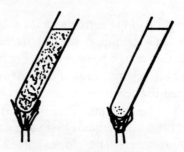

Figure 2.

These operations, fascinating to little children, require nevertheless a certain attention. We are giving them practical information—that sugar crystals are soluble in warm water and not soluble in cold water—at the same time that we are educating their patience.

As for the starch, it remains undissolved even after shaking the tube. Its presence makes the water opaque: it is "in suspension."

Therefore, a solution may be colored but remain transparent

whereas the liquid containing a substance in suspension becomes opaque. The two test tubes just prepared show this clearly.

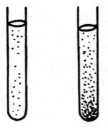

Figure 3.

We now take a blue solution of copper sulfate and water to see if it is possible to free the water of the dissolved substance. In order to filter it, we must first see how to prepare a filter in a funnel, how to attach the paper, and how to measure to prevent the paper being too large for the funnel. The paper must not reach the funnel's rim. For the experiment to be more striking, we first filter the water containing starch. We see that it becomes clear again. We have, in this way, demonstrated the ease with which water may be freed of a substance it contains in suspension. We proceed in the same way with the solution of copper sulfate. We note that the water, although filtered, remains colored. This means that the solution is a liquid that has itself become a new substance.

We have seen that, upon filtering a liquid in which a substance is found to be in suspension, that liquid becomes clear. And yet the substance found in dissolution has not been removed. To remove it, we must boil it. If we do not have the apparatus necessary for distillation we cannot succeed in purifying the water. But we are able to see what remains of the dissolved substance when we have caused the water to evaporate. This operation is called "calcination." We recall the calcium carbonate that remains on the bottom of the sea after the evaporation of the water.

On the other hand, if a deposit remains in the test tube, we are able, though imperfectly in practice, to free the liquid from the deposit by "decantation." These new terms are exact, and we will be able to write them in a book or on separate cards with an explanation of each.

We have the children note that to boil liquids we always place a screen between the flame and the container, which indicates that great care must be taken in order not to burn it when the liquid is entirely evaporated.

This experiment shows that the water has disappeared without having been able to take anything with it. The copper sulfate that remains is a solid which we may remove and again dissolve in water to obtain a second solution as blue as the first. Thus we have been able to remove the substance first found in water and put it into other water.

These exercises are very simple but they require time because it is necessary to wait patiently while the liquids settle, while substances dissolve, or while the liquids evaporate. Calm and attention are required. The psychological effect produced on the children at this age may be compared to that of the silence lesson on the younger children. The small children severely restrict their movements, while the older ones must measure their movements and must therefore pay concentrated attention to them.

We may follow now with another exercise which is neither complicated nor difficult to understand but which requires patience, care, and a steady hand. It consists in filling a test tube with water. When the tube is full to the brim it may be noted, on careful observation, that the surface of the water is concave because the water adheres to the glass. This union is called "cohesion." More difficult yet is the task of adding a small quantity of water to the test tube which is already full. When this has been done it will be seen that the surface of the water has become convex. This phenomenon is caused by the powerful force of cohesion of the water itself. It is for this reason that falling water takes the form of drops—i.e., a spherical form. The drop is simultaneously convex and concave.

We can have the children recall the formation of stalactites and stalagmites. These also fix the children's attention on water.

Let us bring them to discover, through experiment, the principle of communicating receptacles.

We take a U-shaped test tube and explain that the water may come to the surface of the land because it seeks the level of the underground water table. Many springs are the result of the existence of this phenomenon. Thus, to use on one hill the water whose source is on another hill of the same altitude, it is enough to put them in communication. If the Romans had known this principle they would not have built the immense aqueducts we admire. It would have been sufficient for them to connect one point with the other.

Then, too, we have them note that the surface of the water is a horizontal plane. To show this we take a V-shaped test tube. In the oblique arm, the form of the surface of the water is elliptic. In the other, held vertically, the surface is circular. This proves that the surface of a liquid always remains on the horizontal plane. In fact, to find the horizontal, it suffices to let liquid come to rest. From these demonstrations arise principles which allow us to introduce mathematical determinations when we later broach the study of scientific instruments.

Let us speak now of the chemical composition of water. The child needs to know something of a science which has, in our day, taken on such great importance. We cannot yet give him great theories or the exact chemical science; that will come later. But at this age he must receive the seeds which will germinate later. He needs an impression, an idea which above all awakens interest. If he acquires the interest he will later be able to study and understand these subjects rapidly. If the interest is not aroused, the sciences, which have attained such a degree of development and which have so much influence on present-day civilization, will remain obscure.

We must hunt, therefore, for everything that may be accessible to the mind of the child in order to create the bases for future development. That is to say, that we must sow impressions before presenting science. We must here again have recourse to the imagination to create the impressions and to reach conclusions little by little. To do this we must seek the symbols accessible to the child that bait the primitive logic that makes him reason. Nothing can speak to his imagination better than science, because he sees in it a sort of magic. The fact that a body in association with another—as in the case of water —may invisibly form a third reality gives the impression of something magic. The mind awakens in the face of creation.

Hydrogen, the light, invisible gas which seeks to escape, and oxygen, another gas which is always contained in the air—both of which we never see, but which are necessary to us and of which the children have always heard —are breathed by all, even the fish in water. Oxygen is a surprising gas. It is because of it that things burn.

Air is made up of about one-fifth oxygen and about four-fifths nitrogen, which moderates the oxygen. Without it, the oxygen would burn everything. We know nitrogen. We have often heard about nitrified substances. During the war Germany used the nitrogen of the air to obtain explosives. It is curious to note that one gas of which the air is made up burns and that the other explodes. What is more, oxygen and hydrogen unite to give us water.

8

Carbon in Nature

Carbon in Nature

THE PURE air we breathe is soiled by carbon dioxide emitted by the lungs. Carbon dioxide is poisonous to us and to animals. How is it that we have never been asphyxiated? This is another mystery much like that of water. There is an element that maintains the purity of the air and has done so for centuries and centuries since the beginning.

It could be supposed that only hydrogen and oxygen, both invisible, existed; that an explosion occurred; that the cataracts of heaven were opened; and that water had been created. Water is formed of two parts hydrogen and one part oxygen. The water which did not exist before could have been formed suddenly by a spark. It is in fact possible to make water in this way. These experiments should not be done too soon. But the phenomenon may be described as though it were a marvelous tale by explaining how water, which is transparent but may be felt, is formed by two substances both of which are invisible.

And while we are on the subject of the creation of a substance, we inform the child that chemistry is the study of newly created substances. To illustrate, we place a piece of sugar in a flask and pour on it a liquid having the appearance of water—sulfuric acid. We mix the two substances well. Sugar dissolves in water, but in this instance we suddenly see smoke come from the flask. We are present at the formation, as if by magic, of a new substance:

carbon. White sugar is, in substance, a piece of coal. Coal, then, according to its different forms and aspects may have different uses and qualities.

It may be said that all the substances that burn become coal. Trees become coal. The roast forgotten on the fire becomes coal. We, too, are carbon combined with other substances. Coal is found scattered all over. It is a very important substance. The desire to discover certain characteristics of these elements never fails to arise. The small child is already using symbols. The letters of the alphabet are symbols. He has only a small number, but, combined among themselves, they form words, poems. The musical notes are symbols, dots. Music makes us happy, makes us sing and dance. So why would we not be able to symbolize another phenomenon, that of creation?

The four elements we symbolize for the children in this way are, as it were, the key to the universe.

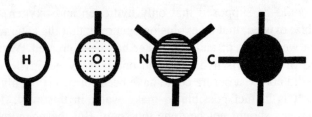

Figure 4.

They are easy to remember because they have 1, 2, 3, and 4 lines. They do, in fact, make us think of keys.

We could depict them in the form of bodies having arms capable of grasping one another. Some elements irresistibly combine (embrace). Thus hydrogen combines with oxygen which, having two arms, is able to hold two hydrogens. Water is represented thus:

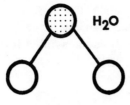

Figure 5.

On the other hand, carbon, which has four arms, uses two of them to attach to each of two oxygens to form carbon dioxide, which is represented:

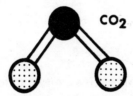

Figure 6.

These two elements are fundamentally important. They could be considered to be the two activators of the universe.

Nitrogen, which has three arms, combines with three hydrogens to form a relatively important compound, ammonia.

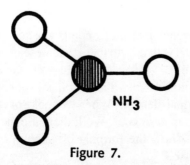

Figure 7.

Ammonia is the ultimate form taken by nitrified substances of an organism in decomposition.

The way in which the elements unite is what maintains the attention of the child. Here is the symbol for nitric acid:

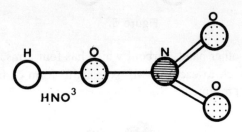

Figure 8.

Nitrogen (in this case) has five arms; with four of them it gets hold of two oxygens which, as we have seen, have two arms each. The last arm of nitrogen takes hold of one arm of another oxygen which, in its turn, unites itself to one hydrogen with its remaining free arm. It is quite difficult for us to use ammonia to make nitric acid. But in nature this occurs constantly. It occurs, however, by means of intermediary living things—microbes, which possess a power we do not have. They separate the hydrogens and replace them with oxygens. If these micro-organisms did not exist, the earth would fill with ammonia and the plants would not find nutrients because they feed on nitrates coming from nitric acid. These micro-organisms, then, contribute to the nutrition of the plants, because it is thanks to them that these chemical transformations take place.

In carbon dioxide, of which we have spoken, it is the carbon that is the principal element. When we spoke of calcium carbonate, it was again a matter of coal. Well, then, are the rocks themselves carbon? Let us show the formula of calcium carbonate, starting with calcium itself:

Figure 9.

Carbon, which has four arms, uses two to hold an oxygen and with the other two arms holds another two oxygens. Each of the latter still has a free arm, with which they grasp the two arms of the calcium.

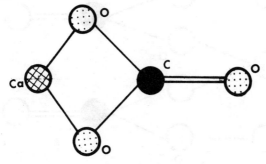

Figure 10.

When rain water, carrying carbonic anhydride, strikes the rocks—which are formed by calcium carbonate—bicarbonate of calcium is formed. This is soluble in water and, consequently, the stone is disaggregated.

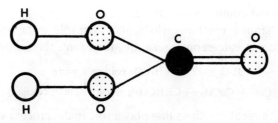

Figure 11..

At the same time the opposite also takes place; that is, new continents are formed. When carbonic anhydride and water are eliminated from bicarbonate of calcium (that is to say, when carbonic acid is eliminated), it is transformed into calcium carbonate. This, being insoluble, brings about the formation of calcareous structures like stalactites, stalagmites, madrepores, and corals and thus the formation of atolls.

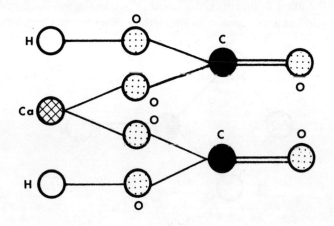

Figure 12.

This is the great drama of nature, thanks to which mountains are decomposed and new lands are formed. This is how water dissolves and continuously creates.

The chemical reactions which play their role in the process of degradation of calcareous rocks are, therefore, the following:

$$H_2O + CO_2 \rightarrow H_2CO_3 \text{ (carbonic acid)}$$

$$H_2CO_3 + CaCO_3 \rightarrow Ca(HCO_3)_2 \text{ (bicarbonate of calcium)}$$

The chemical reactions that play a role in the process whereby calcareous structures are formed are, then, the following:

$$Ca(HCO_3)_2 \rightarrow CO_2 + H_2O + CaCO_3$$

The carbonic anhydride is dispersed into the air during this process. Although the processes of these two cycles (of degradation and formation) do not have any reciprocal relation with each other, the two chemical reactions (of decomposition and composition) which bring about this unceasing and dramatic "cycle of rocks" may be summarized in the single reversible reaction that follows:

$$H_2CO_3 + CaCO_3 \rightarrow Ca(HCO_3)_2$$

It is interesting to be present at what happens among all these elements which one could consider as the keys that command the intimate movements of nature. If these ideas are offered to the child in this simple fashion, he becomes passionately interested to see what happens. And once he has become acquainted with these substances, it becomes easy for him to represent them by means of simple symbols.

9

A Few Ideas of Inorganic Chemistry

A Few Ideas of Inorganic Chemistry

THE POINT of view from which we present to the children these sciences in their embryonic state must be well understood. Our presentation must be sensorial and imaginative, given by means of clear visual symbols which permit details to be determined.

We are trying to arouse the child's interest. Should we fail to arouse it immediately, we must still trust the same principle while we make our presentations in a specific environment and await the reaction. If the enthusiasm is not shown we do not delay but pass on. If the enthusiasm is shown we have apparently opened a door. We are at the beginning of a long road, along which we will travel with the child. But what we would most like to recommend is not to begin too late. Thus, the presentation of chemistry may be made at nine years of age. The interest may even manifest itself sooner.

A question that always exists in our adult minds is whether these problems, which already seem to us to be so difficult, will be well understood by the child. "Will he understand molecules, the atom? Will he understand the formulas?" It seems impossible to us that he will follow the study of atomic theory. But it is not a science we want to bring to him at this time. It is nothing else than a germ capable of arousing interest and which will develop later. We recommend above all not to give too many explanations but rather to give precise names. Here is an anecdote to illustrate this advice: A child asks his father why the leaves are green. Happy to seize the opportunity, the father launches into explanations of chlorophyll, the air, light, seeming never to finish. The child listens politely but thinks: "What a shame to have provoked all that!"

As for the question of the molecule and the atom, we can explain it thus: Let us hunt for the smallest part of something. For example, let us divide a geometric figure in other, always smaller figures until we can go no further. The atom is the part of an element that cannot be divided further. Here is another comparison: "For humanity, the atom is man. If a man be subdivided he is no longer a man." Going from this example we can say: man and woman are two atoms of humanity. A man and a woman together form a molecule. Which is to say that a molecule is composed of at least two parts.

The children, moreover, will not pose these questions because it is the symbolic representations that interest them. What pleases the children about water is that the oxygens and hydrogens wish to remain united and that they seek each other as though driven by a mutual liking for each other. In the same way, carbon unites itself with oxygen to form carbon dioxide.

Hydrogen has only one possibility of uniting, oxygen has two, et cetera. Thus, whether it has 1, 2, 3, or 4 arms, each must seize another element. If the atoms were alone they would unite among themselves so as to be always satisfied. But instead of speaking about "arms," we can now say that the elements have a value of 1, 2, 3, or 4 and that the value is called "valence." Now we say that hydrogen has a valence of 1, that oxygen has a valence of 2, et cetera.

We must have the courage to give as many names as possible. The more difficult the names are, the more attractive they are to the child. And then one may say that hydrogen is univalent, that oxygen is bivalent, et cetera. It is easier to express this concept this way than to speak of 1, 2, or 3 arms.

For all that, it is not in proportion to their valences alone that elements unite. They must also have an affinity which causes them to seek one another. They could be said to have an instinct that pushes them to seek out one rather than another. The secret is in the choice and not in the valences. For this reason we cannot play with elements. The symbols show which substances are present and how a compound is formed. In this way we are brought to write the formula.

When all the valences are saturated, satisfied, the compound is stable.

Two elements cannot unite unless there is affinity. Thus, oxygen and nitrogen—both of which have been present in the atmosphere for centuries and centuries—have not united. It is as though there were present in the atoms an interior force that gives them the possibility of choice. The union corresponds to the power of the valances, which is to say that the characteristics are proper to the atoms themselves. They are driven to choose, to form a stable compound that will be a new substance.

Rock is formed of oxygen, carbon, and calcium. And yet neither marble nor alabaster is oxygen, which is a gas, or carbon, or calcium. It is another material, a new creation, a rock.

All of creation—water, rock—derives from the atoms which seek each other out, unite to each other, and, together, lead to a new creation. It is always the same elements that the atoms seek: the same and not others. The limits are ruled by laws. All the details of creation constitute a marvel which we must not fail to bring to the children's attention.

To this creation, through visual representations of form and color, with the letters of the alphabet or with musical notes, we bring forward the idea of stability. By the help of experiments we are able to be present at the creation of a substance, as we have seen with the coal. This is something absolutely sensorial which arouses the child's interest. There is no need, at present, to penetrate further into the study of inorganic chemistry, to which the study of all mineral compounds belongs.

10

A Few Ideas of Organic Chemistry

A Few Ideas of Organic Chemistry

WE CAN even bring the child some notions of organic chemistry. This is thought today—but this is a mistake—to be more difficult, so much so that it is not taught before the student's entry into the university. But if some formulas of organic chemistry are presented in visual form, why should they be more difficult than the others?

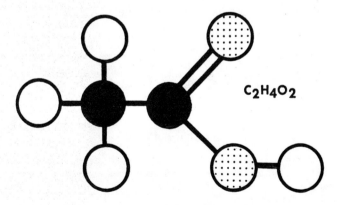

$C_2H_4O_2$

Figure 13.

What, then, is so complicated about this formula, which is that of acetic acid? We can now illustrate also that of butyric acid, which differs from the preceding only in that it has two more carbon brothers.* We then proceed to illustrate palmitic acid, which has a long chain of carbon atoms.

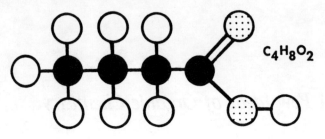

$C_4H_8O_2$

Figure 14.

The OH group is called a "hydroxyl."

We note that carbon, which enters into these organic compounds, is, in a way, the vertebral column and that what revolves around it is simply water. That is all. With the same elements —hydrogen, oxygen, carbon—a number of different combinations can be made.

It is as though a gown were embroidered with different colored threads. What is responsible for the variety is the ingenuity of the embroiderer. It is less a question of the valences—that is, the

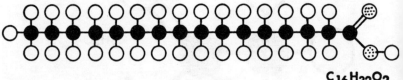

$C_{16}H_{32}O_2$

Figure 15.

*Instead of the formula $C_2H_4O_2$ of acetic acid, the rational version $CH_3–COOH$ is to be preferred as it brings out the functional carbosilic group $COOH$, which characterized saturated nonbasic fatty acids.

So, instead of the formula of butyric (or butanoic) acid C_4HO_2, we may use $C_3H_7–COOH$ or, still better, $CH_3–(CH_2)_2–COOH$. Those formulae render evident the functional group made up of the methylic radical CH_2, which is intermediately repeated.

As far as palmitic acid is concerned, instead of the formula $C_{16}H_{32}O_2$, the rational $C_{15}H_{31}–COOH$ or, as already mentioned, still better $CH_3–(CH_2)_{14}–COOH$, are preferable—*trans*.

different stitches of embroidery—than of the ingenuity, the power, which is to say the work of life. What we note here is the fact that it is not the interior structure of the atoms but rather a force external to them that holds them together in a certain way. It is not the chemical affinity but life that holds them together. Perhaps this concept is difficult, not the formula. The molecules can be very large, so that each molecule may have three hundred or more atoms.

It is necessary to remember that the stability of compounds formed, as a family through the centuries, is a particularity of inorganic chemistry. The particularity of organic chemistry, on the other hand, is the instability of the compounds formed. That is to say, these substances are formed by groups of atoms held together by an exterior force so that the atoms are interchangeable but the type of compound persists.

There are other slightly more complicated formulas in which the atoms of carbon are not present as brothers holding hands. We find carbon and the hydroxyls but we also find a novelty: some atoms of oxygen slip in, as, for example, in this formula for starch:*

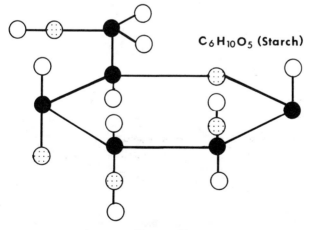

$C_6H_{10}O_5$ (Starch)

Figure 16.

*Figures 16 and 17 are improved versions of those that appeared in an earlier edition—*trans*.

and in this one for glucose:

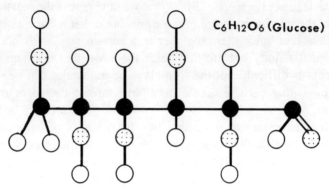

$C_6H_{12}O_6$ (Glucose)

Figure 17.

Here we have a schematic diagram which may be used as an example of correlation. It is a tree with its root, trunk, branches, and leaves.

Figure 18.

The action of which we have already spoken takes place in all its parts. The tree, in fact, takes its nourishment from the ground through its roots. Chemistry permits us to discover that the roots of the tree absorb nutritive substances, of which water and nitrogen are the two main ones. But the nitrogen, in order to constitute a nutritive substance, must be found in a special chemical composition. This poses an essential problem. What is it that furnishes the nitrogen which the plants require continually and which they absorb? What or who replaces this nitrogen in the ground? Nothing in nature may be touched upon without this problem arising.

All living beings need something or someone to help them to live. And here rises before us the problem of the secret of nature, so important in education.

The organic substances that are no longer alive fall to the ground. If the organic substances are no longer alive, the force that kept the atoms together as large molecules no longer exists. So the molecules break up, the atoms detach and follow their instincts: carbon takes two oxygens away with it, et cetera.

In this way the organic compounds become inorganic, with the help of infinitely small beings. Very little remains of the living beings: a little carbon dioxide, a little ammonia, and a little water. The organic substances disappear. All this work of disintegration takes place in the ground.

One day in Rome I was present at the exhumation of the remains in a paupers' cemetary, an operation which takes place every ten years in order to reclaim space. I saw the workers dig without finding more than the occasional bit of debris. They were digging in beautiful black, clean soil, a good, healthy, odorless soil.

Plants absorb these nitrified organic substances from the earth through their roots. Ammonia remains behind. The plants cannot absorb it in this form. It is necessary, then, for the compounds of nitrogen and hydrogen to change to compounds having oxygen. This is very difficult to reproduce in chemistry laboratories. But in nature, microbes in the ground devote themselves to this task continually. From this work arise the nitrites and nitrates which the plants can absorb. Without the microbes this passage from death to life would not exist. When all the organic substances have disappeared, carbon dioxide, water, and nitrogen remain. The nitrogen is changed and the plants may then absorb it.

Green leaves are found at the other end of the tree. The substance responsible for their color is chlorophyll. The role of chlorophyll is to absorb carbon dioxide—a poison continually emitted by all animals and even by the earth—from the air and to decompose it: to retain the carbon and to allow the oxygen to escape. The tree thus becomes a veritable storehouse of carbon. We know this is so because we use wood to obtain warmth. We also know that tree fossils constitute storehouses of carbon. This is why leaves are necessary for the absorption of carbon and the purification of the air.

But chlorophyll all alone would not be able to complete this task. Collaboration is necessary in the form of the sun's rays. Even the tree would not be able to accomplish its great task alone if it were not for the other force independent of it—solar energy.

The tree then is a link, on the one hand to invisible microbes, and on the other hand to the sun. Many good and beautiful things owe their existence to the contact with microbes: flowers and fruits. . . . How generous the tree is! How hard it works! It prepares carbon. It purifies the air. It gives us fruit. It gives us flowers. All the plants cause this thought to arise. Even plants more modest than the tree devote themselves to this useful task and as veritable industrialists they prepare nutritive substances. We mention potatoes, wheat, starch, beets, sugar cane, etc.

That is the nature of creation.

We see that the plants devote themselves to the tasks proper to them just as do the corals that construct a continent. They are workers who draw their nourishment and seek the best conditions of life. That is the cycle of life, as we have seen the cycle of rock. All living beings are destined to contribute to the well-being of other living beings. It is difficult to establish a parallel between the phenomena of nature and those of human life. But a parallel does exist, and principally because men, as a group, must have a great task in creation, although on a level considerably higher than that of nature. Each man works for other men. Industry and commerce may be considered as an active relationship comparable to those found in nature. Could we not restudy the history of humanity from this new point of view?

If we examine nature and the supranature constructed by man side by side, all that belongs to the former elucidates what happens in the latter.

The difference between the constitution of vegetable cells and animal cells may also be noted.

Plant cells are rectangular, or, better, prismatic. Their membranes are thick, strong, and only slightly permeable. They give an impression of the strength of vegetables and the power of their defense. Also, as they grow they spread in all directions. They are characterized by branching. Their roots fix themselves in the ground to hold them secure. They absorb the sun's rays, particularly through the leaves. The plant is beautiful and clean. It sports many colors and scents. Its roots transform ugliness into beauty.

Animals begin their cycle as spheroid cells, the membrane of which, being very fine, very light, seems to be in continual danger. Timid of aspect, they limit themselves, unlike the plant cells, and do not invade the space without. As they grow they fold back over themselves in one, two, or more layers. The complexity of their functions is always found on the inside. In addition, the animal is unable to obtain the substances for his nourishment without moving about to procure them.

Which of the two has superior characteristics? The animals are considered to be on a higher level of nature, and yet we usually consider the characteristics of the plants superior. The animals give the impression of being humble, without defense, always moving, buffeted here and there. And yet we say that the animal is superior for that very reason. We call it "animal" because there is something within it that guides it and makes it move. In continual danger, it must always hunt its own nourishment. It depends on the vegetable world, be it for food or for the purification of the air it breathes. It never has the purity of the vegetable, which is always clean. It could be thought that the animal is always in battle against the vegetable world, and yet the two forms are necessary to each other and give mutual assistance to each other.

Interest now begins to mount with regard to human behavior. Nature reveals that he who is truly a superior and strong being is he who, in spite of weakness, always gains the upper hand.

11

Conclusion

Conclusion

ALL OF what we have just suggested is, in reality, only an example for the application of the method. But we would like to help the child to reach loftier conceptions. What must first be understood is our aim, which is to follow as nearly as possible, as all-inclusively as possible, the needs of growth and of life.

We have touched on several cycles, as, for example, that of calcium carbonate. But all is inter-related. And what is interesting is to be able to orient ourselves among these correlations. To present detached notions is to bring confusion. We need to determine the bonds that exist between them. When the correlation among the notions, by now linked one to the other, has been established, the details may be found to tie together among themselves. The mind, then, is satisfied and the desire to go on with research is born.

Then, by determining the correlation between things with the child, and thereby obeying an essential impulse of the human mind, we create a philosophy for him. And why may not the child philosophize?

Since the human mind is mathematical and philosophic, we try, in reasonable proportions, to turn it toward mathematics and philosophy.

Here then is an essential principle of education: to teach details is to bring confusion; to establish the relationship between things is to bring knowledge.*

*For further reading: Dr. Maria Montessori's *The Montessori Elementary Material* (New York: Schocken Books, 1973) and *To Educate the Human Potential* (Madras, India: Kalakshetra Publications, 1967).

APPENDICES

APPENDICES

*"Erdkinder"**

GENERAL CONSIDERATIONS

THE NEED THAT is so keenly felt for a reform of secondary schools concerns not only an educational, but also a human and social problem. This can be summed up in one sentence: Schools as they are today, are adapted neither to the needs of adolescence nor to the times in which we live. Society has not only developed into a state of utmost complication and extreme contrasts, but it has now come to a crisis in which the peace of the world and civilization itself are threatened. The crisis is certainly connected with the immense progress that has been made in science and its practical applications, but it has not been caused by them. More than to anything else it is due to the fact that the development of man himself has not kept pace with that of his external environment.

While material progress has been extremely rapid and social life has been completely transformed, the schools have remained in a kind of arrested development, organized in a way that cannot have been well suited even to the needs of the past, but that today is actually in contrast with human progress. The reform of the secondary school may not solve all the problems of our times, but it is certainly a necessary step, and a practical, though limited, contribution to an urgently needed reconstruction of society. Everything that concerns education assumes today an importance of a

*Land-children

general kind, and must represent a protection and a practical aid to the development of man; that is to say, it must aim at improving the individual in order to improve society.

But, above all it is the education of adolescents that is important, because adolescence is the time when the child enters on the state of manhood and becomes a member of society. If puberty is on the physical side a transition from an infantile to an adult state, there is also, on the psychological side, a transition from the child who has to live in a family, to the man who has to live in society. These two needs of the adolescent: for protection during the time of the difficult physical transition, and for an understanding of the society which he is about to enter to play his part as a man, give rise to two problems that are of equal importance concerning education at this age.

If we must specify which of the social circumstances of our time has the greatest effect on the problems that we are considering, we should say that it is the fact that the future seems insecure and full of unknown factors. The material world is in the process of rapid evolution and contains the dangers and uncertainties of a new adjustment. We have lost that "security" which we had in the past; we need only think of the difference between the times when crafts were handed on peacefully from father to son, and the confusion of sudden, unexpected demands that causes the necessity for "vocational guidance" and re-training. Equally in the field of manual work, as in the intellectual professions (although somewhat later there), that certainty of a good post is lost, which should be the reward of completed studies and a special training. Such an assured future can no longer be provided for the young people by the family as it used to be in the past. The state, at present, is no longer certain, of ensuring the future employment of those citizens destined to superior professions in the same way as it did in the past, by providing unilateral, exclusive, schools with specialized training. Nowadays it must foresee new difficulties arising from the insecurity of modern conditions. The world is partly in a state of disintegration and partly in a state of reconstruction. It is the alternation of progress and regression that produces this characteristic instability. The world is like a piece of land that is going through the vicissitudes of a settlement of the soil.

Such being the condition of society, we ought to remember that there is one thing that education can take as a sure guide, and that is the *personality of the children* who are to be educated.

It is necessary that the human personality should be prepared for the unforeseen, not only for the conditions that can be anticipated by prudence and foresight. Nor should it be strictly conditioned by one rigid specialization, but should develop at the same time the power of adapting itself quickly and easily. In this fierce battle of civil life a man must have a strong character and quick wits as well as courage; he must be strengthened in his principles by moral training and he must also have practical ability in order to face the difficulties of life. *Adaptability*—this is the most essential quality; for the progress of the world is continually opening new careers, and at the same time closing or revolutionizing the traditional types of employment.

This does not mean that in secondary schools, there should be no preparation for the intellectual professions, and still less that "culture" should be neglected. On the contrary, education must be very wide and very thorough, and not only in the case of the professional intellectuals, but for all men who are living at a time that is characterized by the progress of science and its technical applications. Now, even laborers need education. They must understand the complex problems of our times, otherwise they are just a pair of hands acting without seeing what relation their work has in the pattern of society. Such as they are today, they may be said to have no head. Meanwhile, the intellectuals of today are all cripples as long as their hands remain useless. Their spirit will dry up if the grandeur of the practical reality of our days is completely shut away from them, as if it did not exist. Men with hands and no head, and men with head and no hands are equally out of place in the modern community.

The problem of reforming the secondary schools will not be solved by cutting down "culture," nor by losing sight of the necessity of training for the intellectual professions. But it is essential that this training should not turn out men who have been lulled to sleep by a false sense of security, who are incapable of confronting the unforeseen difficulties of real life, and who are totally ignorant of conditions in the world in which they are destined to live. Not long ago outdoor sports were introduced in order to provide physical exercise for the young people who were leading shut-in, sedentary lives; so, today, there is a need for a more dynamic training of character and the development of a clearer consciousness of social reality.

The secondary schools as they are at present constituted do not concern themselves with anything but the preparation for a career, as if the social conditions of the time were still peaceful and secure. They do not take any special care for the personality of the children, nor do they give all the special physical attention that is necessary during the period of adolescence. Thus not only do they not correspond to the social conditions of our day, but they fail to protect the principal energy on which the future depends: human energy, the power of individual personality. Young people in the secondary schools are compelled to study as a "duty" or a "necessity." They are not working with interest nor any definite aims that could be immediately fulfilled and would give them satisfaction and a renewed interest in continuous effort. They are directed by an external and illogical compulsion, and all their best individual energy is wasted. Adolescents and young people almost right up to maturity are treated like babies in the elementary schools. At fourteen or sixteen they are still subjected to the petty threat of "bad marks" with which the teachers weigh up the work of boys and girls by a method that is just like that of measuring the material weight of lifeless objects with the mechanical aid of a balance. The work is "measured" like inanimate matter, not "judged" as a product of life.

And on these marks the future of the student depends. So study becomes a heavy and crushing load that burdens the young life instead of being felt as the privilege of initiation to the knowledge that is the pride of our civilization. The young people, the men of the future, are formed into a mold of narrowness, artificiality and egotism. What a wretched life of endless penance, of futile renun-ciation of their dearest aspirations!

Another remark to be made of the secondary schools as they are at present constituted is that they hinder the physical development of the adolescents. The period of life in which physical maturity is attained is a delicate and difficult time, because of the rapid development and change which the organism must go through. The human organism becomes so delicate that doctors consider this time to be comparable to the period of birth and rapid growth in the first years thereafter. There exists a particular predisposition to certain diseases and certain forms of weakness, that are collec-tively referred to as "adolescent complaints." The predisposition to tuberculosis is a special danger during the transition from childhood to the adult stage.

From the psychological viewpoint also this is a critical age. There are doubts and hesitations, violent emotions, discourage-ment and an unexpected decrease of intellectual capacity. The difficulty of studying with concentration is not due to a lack of willingness, but is really a psychological characteristic of the age. The assimilative and memorizing powers of the intellect that give young children such an interest in details and in material objects seem to change their nature. The chief symptom of adolescence is a state of expectation, a tendency towards creative work and a need for the strengthening of self-confidence. Suddenly the child be-comes very sensitive to the rudeness and humiliations that he had previously suffered with patient indifference. These reactions, bitter rebellious feelings, sometimes give rise to characters that are morally abnormal; while this is the time, the "sensitive period" when there should develop the most noble characteristics that would prepare a man to be social, that is to say, a sense of justice and a sense of personal dignity. It is just because this is the time when the social man is created, but has not yet reached full development, that in this epoch practically every defect in adjust-ment to social life originates. These defects may have very danger-ous results, either for the future of the individual (timidity, anxi-ety, depression, inferiority complex), or for society (incapacity to work, laziness, dependence on others, or cynicism and criminality). And all these dangers that spring from the very nature of man become still more serious at a time when social life is so disturbed and uncertain as it is at present.

There are therefore two different groups of difficulties that must be considered:

1. Those concerning the present form of society.
2. Those concerning the vital needs of the adolescent.

Life must not remain an "unknown quantity" so that the eventual orphan feels lost, or the immigrant has to seek his safety in the exercise of his one special capacity, in despair when its application may be impossible. For success in life depends in every case on self-confidence and the knowledge of one's own capacity and many-sided powers of adaption. The consciousness of knowing how to make oneself useful, how to help mankind in many ways, fills the soul with noble confidence, with almost religious dignity. The feeling of independence must be bound to the power to be self-sufficient, not a vague form of liberty deducted from the help afforded by the gratuitous benevolence of others. There are two "faiths" that can uphold man: faith in God and faith in himself. And these two faiths should exist side by side: the first belongs to the inner life of man, the second to his life in society.

REFORMS THAT ARE IN RELATION WITH THE SOCIAL LIFE OF TODAY

The essential reform is this: to put the adolescent on the road to achieving economic independence. We might call it a "school of experience in the elements of social life."

This "independence" has more educational than practical value; that is to say, it has a closer connection with the psychology of the adolescent than with an eventual actual utility. So, even if a boy were so rich that his economic security seemed above all the vicissitudes of life he would still derive great personal benefit from being initiated in economic independence. For this would result in a "valorization" of his personality, in making him feel himself capable of succeeding in life by his own efforts and on his own merits, and at the same time it would put him in direct contact with the supreme reality of social life. We speak therefore of letting him earn money by his own work. If we believe that receiving alms is beneath the dignity of a man, and in our modern institutions we give the beggar the chance of earning what he receives, why should the same principle not be applied to the young people who are receiving the benefit of education.

But the word "work" must have a particular interpretation in this case. The expression "work for wages" at once suggests a trade and implies technical training and competition. This work should, instead, be an exercise of "utilized virtues," of "super-values" and skills acquired beyond the limits of one's own particular specialization, past or future.

This conception of work implies a general principle that holds the work itself to be of greater importance than the kind of work. All work is noble, the only ignoble thing is to live without working. There is need to realize the value of work in all its forms, whether manual or intellectual, to be called "mate," to have a sympathetic understanding of all forms of activity. Education should therefore include the two forms of work, manual and intellectual, for the same person, and thus make it understood by practical experience that these two kinds complete each other and are equally essential to a civilized existence.

This directly educative conception differs from a somewhat analogous practice that has existed for a long time in modern American schools, both secondary schools and universities, that is called "self-help." This began with the work of a woman, Mary Lyons, in 1837 and has the exclusively practical purpose of making it possible for poor students of good will who want to be taught to earn with their own work the fees for their tuition, instead of having to depend on scholarships which are necessarily limited in number. This practical plan, which enables a larger number of intelligent people to have the benefit of advanced education, has been put into operation by the schools themselves and makes a direct contribution to the benefit of youth. That is to say, the school itself obtains, allocates, supervises, and safeguards the work done as self-help. This work is found either within the school itself, which is easy where the school is residential, or else outside the school, but in some of the occupations that are connected with school-organization. This plan has developed very greatly in the schools of the United States; it is an experiment that has been crowned with success.

Self-help has shown two things:

1. that it has great moral value because it "rouses the conscience from the inertia" in which it is generally found among young people who are being passively maintained by their families, and it teaches in a practical way the value of time and of their own powers.

2. that the work does not hinder study, but even makes it possible to study better; in fact the students who are obliged to resort to self-help are generally those who turn out the best and most successful scholars.

We can therefore cite the success of this experiment in support of our assertion that productive work and a wage that gives economic independence, or rather constitutes a first real attempt to achieve economic independence, could be made with advantage a general principle of social education for adolescents and young people.

If we consider the plan from the point of view of our own method it can be regarded as a development of that principle that has already had such great success in our schools for smaller children right down to the nursery class, known as the "exercises of practical life." The children of three years of age in the "Children's Houses" learn and carry out such work as sweeping, dusting, making things tidy, setting the table for meals, waiting at table, washing the dishes, etc., and at the same time they learn to attend to their own personal needs, to wash themselves, to take showers, to comb their hair, to take a bath, to dress and undress themselves, to hang up their clothes in the wardrobe, or to put them in drawers, to polish their shoes. These exercises are part of the method of education, and do not depend on the social position of the pupils; even in the "Children's Houses" attended by rich children who are given every kind of assistance at home, and who are accustomed to being surrounded by a crowd of servants, take part in the exercises of practical life. This has a truly educational, not utilitarian purpose. The reaction of the children may be described as a "burst of independence" of all unnecessary assistance that suppresses their activity and prevents them from demonstrating their own capacities. It is just these "independent" children of ours who learn to write at the age of four and a half years, who learn to read spontaneously, and who amaze everyone by their progress in arithmetic.

These children seem to be precocious in their intellectual development and they demonstrate that while working harder than other children they do so without tiring themselves. These very children revealed to us the most vital need of their development, saying: *"Help me to do it alone!"*

Independence, in the case of the adolescents, has to be acquired on a different plane, for theirs is the economic independence in the field of society. Here, too, the principle of "Help me to do it alone!" ought to be applied.

This is not absolute independence. It is very like the state of the man who, feeling himself dependent on God, must still try to act, saying as if in a prayer for his own human weakness: "Help me to do it alone!"

REFORMS RELATING TO THE VITAL NEEDS OF ADOLESCENCE

The essential reform of our plan from this point of view may be defined as follows: during the difficult time of adolescence it is helpful to leave the accustomed environment of the family in the town and go to quiet surroundings in the country, close to nature. Here, an open-air life, individual care, and a non-toxic diet, must be the first considerations in organizing a "center for study and work."

This theory is based on a plan that has been experimentally adopted all over the world, the custom of having boarding schools (secondary schools for adolescents) situated in places far from the large cities, in the country or in small towns. These boarding schools have sprung up in England in great numbers and for all classes, even the most privileged (Eton and Harrow) and the same type is found in the universities of Oxford and Cambridge. Such institutions were so successful in England and the United States that, as everyone knows, towns were built up round the universities that were previously isolated. This is the case with the majority of the modern universities in America. The proposal we have put forward has, therefore, nothing surprising about it, and there is no need of further experiment to establish the practical value of this principle. Life in the open air, in the sunshine, and a diet high in nutritional content coming from the produce of neighboring fields improve the physical health, while the calm surroundings, the silence, the wonders of nature satisfy the need of the adolescent mind for reflection and meditation. Further, in a college, the whole order of the daily life can be made to suit the demands of study and work, whereas the routine of family life has first to conform to the needs of the parents.

But our plan is not simply a reproduction of the ordinary boarding school in the country or small town. For it is not the country itself that is so valuable, but work in the country, and work generally, with its wide social connotations of productiveness and earning power. The observation of nature has not only a side that is philosophical and scientific, it has also a side of social experiences that leads on to the observations of *civilization* and the *life of men*.

By work in the country we do not mean that the students should be obliged to work like agricultural laborers. The intensive methods of modern agriculture produce wonders as great as nature itself. The improvement on nature produced not by labor alone, but by the inventiveness of man with the help of the sciences, appears to be a kind of ''supercreation'' due to the labor of civilization. The first stage of civilization is just that of the transformation of nature to a higher level of beauty and usefulness in her products, and of an apparently miraculous use of the secrets of nature. This is truly a "supra-nature" devised by man. This supra-nature includes the great scientific progress in biology and in chemistry, and a consecutive progress of succeeding generations that makes one wonder at the greatness of man as well as the greatness of God.

Therefore work on the land is an introduction both to nature and to civilization and gives a limitless field for scientific and historic studies. If the produce can be used commercially this brings in the fundamental mechanism of society, that of production and exchange, on which economic life is based. This means that there is an opportunity to learn both academically and through actual experience what are the elements of social life.

We have called these children the "Erdkinder" because they are learning about civilization through its origin in agriculture. They are the "land-children." They are learning of the beginning of civilization that occurred when the tribes settled on the land and began a life of peace and progress while the nomads remained barbarians and warriors. An immense ideal: that of civilization that unfolds in the environment of nature ought to uplift the kind of life to be led by these "novices of society." Just as nature is brought by the labor of man to a higher degree of beauty and usefulness, so man must raise himself to a state that is higher than his natural state, and the land-child must see that society is in a state of ascent from nature in which he, as a civilized and religious man must play his part.

The school where the children live, or rather their country homes, can also give them the opportunity for social experience, for it is an institution organized on a larger scale and with greater freedom than the family. This organization could take the form of a private hotel as far as the management and control are concerned. In some ways it could be regarded as a real hotel, or the "land-children's hostel." By taking part in the administration the young people could gain experience of hotel-keeping in all its various branches, of organizing for comfort and order and the least effort in maintenance, of countless other responsibilities and of the financial side. Indeed, if little children are capable of keeping the house clean and tidy, of waiting at table, of washing dishes, of taking care of small pottery, etc., the adolescents can easily learn to run a hotel; a career which nowadays has special schools of instruction. The hotel-keeping can also be extended from their own hostel to other simple "hotels" where the relations of the student could come to stay for a few days to find out how their children are living. By choosing this place to spend a short and pleasant holiday, parents and others could make a contribution towards the economic support of the institution.

The hotel run on modern lines, with artistic simplicity and with gaiety and free from artificial constraint, should provide an interesting and pleasant form of occupation, and an opportunity for developing good taste and efficiency in domestic matters.

Finally we should like to suggest another institution which might become of great importance, and that is the shop. A shop or store could be established in the nearest big town, and here the land-children could easily bring and sell the produce of their fields and garden and other things that they had made. Eventually they might also collect and bring things made by other people who are poor and know some craft and can produce pretty or useful objects of which they could not dispose commercially in the usual way. This would be real social work and would encourage those small village industries that are being lost today through the prevalence of machinery and mass production. This trade could have a special effect in preserving something of a past age when personality could be expressed in the construction of the simplest objects.

The shop itself could be regarded as a revival of the medieval exchange that was a general meeting place and social center, beautifully decorated and blessed and consecrated by religion, and where buying and selling were conducted with scrupulous honesty. This was also a place where the small tradesman could make those individual bargains that are also the beginnings of acquaintance and the foundation of friendship and social life. In times gone by, the churches themselves were places of business, and so were the streets, where the scanty traffic left enough space for goods to be exposed for sale when only small transactions were made.

Many reminders still exist of the old custom of mixing up trade with friendship and personal contacts. And this custom could be re-established by the young people with their happiness, enthusiasm, and their desire for every kind of experience.

The shop would also necessitate a genuine study of commerce and exchange, of the art of ascertaining the demand and being ready to meet it, of the strict and rigid rules of bookkeeping. But the thing that is important above everything else is that the adolescent should have a life of *activity* and *variety*, and that one occupation should act as a "holiday" from another occupation. The shop would be in respect to the studies of economics and politics an educational object, similar to the aquarium or terrarium in the case of the study of biology.

B

Study and Work Plans

PLAN OF STUDIES AND WORK

It is impossible to fix a priori a detailed program for study and work. We can only give the general plan. This is because a program should only be drawn up gradually under the guidance of experience.

Study need not be restricted by the curricula of existing secondary schools and still less need we make use of their methods of dealing with the children or instilling culture. We must say at once that the aim should be to *widen* education instead of restricting it. Our reform is one of the distribution of culture and methods of teaching.

The plan aims above all at "valorization of the personality" in the present social conditions. It should not be restricted to consider exclusively the specialized training that will ensure a well-paid post in the future. It is quite obvious that the necessity for such specialization exists and must be considered, but only as a *means*, as a practical method of becoming a member of society, not as an end to which must be sacrificed both the values of the individual and his feeling of responsibility towards society as a whole.

There are two principles to be considered:

1. That for rest it is not necessary to resort to "holidays," which are a waste of time and break the continuity of life. Holidays or rest are simply a change of occupation and surroundings, and this can be provided by a variety of occupations and interests.

2. That study is the response to a need of the intelligence and if based upon our psychic nature, it does not weary, but refreshens and strengthens the mind during its development.

These two principles have been already demonstrated in the "Children's Houses" where the work and study did not result in fatigue, but in an increase of energy so marked that these indefatigable children were found to be working at home as well as at school. (The hours in the first "Children's Houses" were from eight in the morning until six in the evening, yet the children would take away the material from the school so that they could continue to work at home.) This should be found all the more among young people, with immense advantage, both for culture and education. To obtain such a result it is necessary to keep close to nature to assist it by responding to the special needs of development that are experienced at different ages and therefore to consider separately:

1. The moral and physical care of the pupils;
2. The syllabus and methods of studies.

Moral and Physical Care of Boys and Girls

Moral care here refers to the relation between the children, the teachers, and the environment. The teachers must have the greatest respect for the young personality, realizing that in the soul of the adolescent, great values are hidden, and that in the minds of these boys and girls there lies all our hope of future progress and the judgement of ourselves and our times. The intimate vocation of MAN is the secret of the adolescent. If social progress is realized through the succession of the generations, then these children, as they grow up, will become more highly developed than their adult teachers. In every boy there can be seen a reflection of the picture of Jesus in the Temple who amazed the old men with his wisdom, and who forgot his earthly parents in the realization of his bond with a Father in Heaven. But the rest of the story must not be forgotten either: "And he went down with them and came to Nazareth, and was subject unto them" while he was preparing for his future mission.

This respect for the children is of the greatest importance and must be observed in practice. The adolescent must never be treated as a child, for that is a stage of life that he has surpassed. It is better to treat an adolescent as if he had greater value than he actually shows than as if he had less and let him feel that his merits and self-respect are disregarded.

Young people must have enough freedom to allow them to act on individual initiative. But in order that individual action should be free and useful at the same time it must be restricted within certain limits and rules that give the necessary guidance. These rules and restrictions must be those of the whole institution, not forced on separate individuals as though they had no sense of responsibility and were incapable of conforming of their own free will to necessary regulations. The rules must be just those that are necessary and sufficient to maintain order and ensure progress.

The organization must be determined because it is necessary to develop the power of self-adjustment to the environment as it is found, and this adaption results in cooperation and a happy social life that will facilitate individual progress. The environment must make the free choice of occupation easy, and therefore eliminate the waste of time and energy in following vague and uncertain preferences. From all this the result will be not only self-discipline but a proof that self-discipline is an aspect of individual liberty and the chief factor of success in life.

A very important matter is the fundamental order in the succession of occupations during the day, and the times for the "change-over." This should be experimental at first and develop into an established thing; necessities will arise and will have to be dealt with and this will tend to create an organization. But is it necessary to consider not only the active occupations but the need for solitude and quiet, which are essential for the development of the hidden treasures of the soul.

The physical care must include special attention to the physiological condition of adolescence. This is a time of crisis during which all the glands of internal secretion are affected, and, through them, the whole organism. The body is growing rapidly but not at a uniform rate, and this results in a disturbance of functional equilibrium. In the first period the legs are growing far more quickly than anything else, especially the body and chest, and there is consequently a strain on the heart and lungs that results in palpitations and diminished pulmonary resistance. Nor has the muscular strength developed in proportion to the height due to the increase in the length of the legs. It is possible to divide the period of physical adolescence roughly into three periods:

1. development of the legs,
2. development of the body, especially the chest,
3. development of muscular strength.

As these changes take place in short successive periods of about two years it is a good thing to watch the growth of the adolescent, to take anthropometrical measurements and to examine the heart and lungs periodically even when the boy or girl appears to be perfectly healthy.

Special attention must be given to the diet. A non-toxic food rich in vitamins and sugar is suitable for this age. Food should be plentiful and nourishing, but no meat should be given, only vegetarian products, including raw vegetables and especially fruit, accompanied by milk, milk derivates, and eggs. Home-grown vegetables and fruit that have thoroughly ripened on the tree are treasures that can only be had by those who live in the country. The stale vegetables and artificially ripened fruit that are obtainable in the towns are far less valuable and do not contain all that is needed.

The poisons of common consumption, alcohol and nicotine, must be withheld from the adolescent; in their place sweets may be allowed, for sugar is a very important food, as it is in the case of small children.

Life in the open air and sunshine, bathing and swimming, must be made use of to the greatest possible extent, as if in a sanatorium.

For the time when the body is underdeveloped it is better to live in flat country where long walks may be taken, either by the sea or in the woods, rather than in hilly country: not that it is bad in itself, but there is a danger of straining the heart by climbing.

EDUCATION: SYLLABUS AND METHODS

The educational syllabus can be drawn up on a general plan that divides it into three parts:

1. The opening up of ways of expression, which through exercises and external aids will help the difficult development of the personality.

2. The fulfilment of those fundamental needs that we believe to be "formative forces" in the evolution of the soul of man.

3. The theoretical knowledge and practical experience that will make the individual a part of the civilization of the day (general education).

Part One: The Opportunities for Self-Expression.

For this purpose there would be all kinds of artistic occupations open to free choice both as to the time and the nature of the work. Some must be for the individual and some would require the cooperation of a group. They would involve artistic and linguistic ability and imagination, including:

Music: Auditions where the children learn to recognize the composition, its composer, and the period, as is done in literary studies. Choral singing. Practice in playing instruments, both solo and in orchestras.

Language: Diction, elocution. Acting of stories or poems. Practice in making speeches and in logically presenting ideas, debates, and discussions. Practice in public speaking so as to be audible and hold the attention of the audience. Open discussions where they can present their own ideas.

Art: Drawing. Modelling (in plasticine, etc.) either for: Ornamental design, reproduction of nature, creative work of the imagination. This work is not to be considered as a proper training in art, but a means of giving expression to individual esthetic feeling with special reference to handwork and to the learning of modern techniques.

Part Two: Education in Relation to Psychic Development.

The "formative" education that will construct firm foundations for the character consists of three subjects: moral education, mathematics, and languages.

Moral Education is the source of that spiritual equilibrium on which everything else depends and which may be compared to the physical equilibrium or sense of balance without which it is impossible to stand upright or to move into any other position.

Mathematics are necessary because intelligence today is no longer natural but mathematical, and without development and education in mathematics it is impossible to understand or take any part in the special forms of progress characteristic of our times. A person without mathematical training today is like an illiterate in the times when everything depended on literary culture. But even in the natural state the human mind has a mathematical bent, tending to be exact, to take measurements and make comparisons, and to use its limited powers to discover the nature of the various "effects" that nature presents to man while she conceals from him the world of causes. Because of this vital importance of mathematics the school must use special methods for teaching it and make clear and comprehensible its elements with the help of plenty of apparatus that demonstrates the "materialized abstractions" of mathematics.

Language: The development of language is part of the development of the personality, for words are the natural means of expressing thoughts and establishing understanding between men. In the past one language was enough, but today it is a social convention that education should include the ability to read and write correctly in several languages.

Part Three: Education as the Preparation for Adult Life.

General education may be classified in three groups:

1. *The study of the earth and of living things*, that is geology, geography (including the prehistoric periods), biology and cosmology, botany, zoology, physiology, astronomy, comparative anatomy.

2. *The study of human progress and the building up of civilization* in connection with physics and chemistry, mechanics, engineering, genetics. The instruction given must be scientifically correct and must be related to simple everyday facts so that it can always be tested and confirmed by observation or experiment. From this basis it will become possible to understand more complicated matters that cannot be demonstrated in the school. The theory should alternate with the practical work in order to give it wider application and make it more interesting.

The school should possess a "museum of machinery." The machines must be of suitable size so that the children can take them down and reassemble them, also use and repair them. A philosophical reflection arises from this; that is, that machines have given man powers far greater than are natural to him, and that man can only develop as he advances in his work of developing civilization. The man of "supra-natural" powers can see, through lenses, things that are minutely small or remotely distant, and can calculate mathematically, through a "supra-natural" or artificial development of his brain, the exact nature of events that are completely inaccessible and even unimaginable to primitive man. So, today, man can listen to voices that come from tremendous distances and can measure the waves that make these communications possible.

Through machinery man can exert tremendous powers, almost as fantastic as if he were the hero of a fairy tale. Through machinery man can travel with an ever increasing velocity, he can fly through the air and go beneath the surface of the ocean. So that civilized man is becoming more and more "supra-natural" and the social environment progresses correspondingly. If education does not help a man to take part in this "supra-natural" world he must remain an "extra-social" being. The "supra-natural" man is the king of the earth, of all things visible and invisible, he penetrates the secrets of life growing new flowers and breeding new animals that are supercreations, increasing through chemistry the natural produce of the earth, transforming things as though by magical powers. These are the proofs of the greatness of collective humanity: each man may add something to them. But works of art are the products of the genius of isolated individuals, gifted with natural powers superior to those of other men.

These and other similar ideas that will awaken a realization of the power of man and the greatness of civilization should be presented in a form that will stir genuine emotion, for feelings of this kind should exist today together with the feelings of religion and patriotism. For in our times science has created a new world in which the whole of humanity is joined together by a universal scientific culture. Thus, children should learn to use machines habitually as part of their education.

The machine is like an extra adaptable limb of modern man; it is the slave of civilization. But beware, for the man of ill-will may be rendered dangerous by machinery; his influence may become unlimited as the speed of communication increases. Therefore a new morality, individual and social, must be our chief consideration in this new world. This morality must give us new ideas about good and evil, and the responsibilities towards humanity that individuals incur when they assume powers so much greater than those with which they are naturally endowed.

3. *The study of the history of mankind*. This should be treated as far as possible as a complete whole, from which special periods can be chosen for individual study. The available material should include a library of books on the subject, geographical atlases, and a history museum containing pictures, portraits, reproductions of historical documents and prehistoric objects.

The part of history that is most important during the first period of adolescence is the history of scientific discoveries and of geographical explorations. Accounts should be given of the most important inventions accompanied by pictures of social life before and after the discovery. This would show how men have improved through civilization.

Another aspect of history (suitable during the next period) is that which deals with the effect on humanity of the geographical environment, of contact between different peoples, of the intermarriage of races, and the assimilation of special cultures. The wars and conquests of empires should be studied in relation to their ideals and moral standards, and the influence of religion and patriotism on human behavior should be observed. These studies should consider that uplifting of the inner life of humanity towards tendencies that grow ever-less in cruelty and violence and strive to form ever-wider groups of associated individuals.

Besides these general reviews of the subject a detailed study should be made of one period, event, or the life of some personage who has aroused special interest. This would involve the consultation and comparison of documents, chronicles, and portraits until a real understanding of the subject has been achieved.

In addition, a special study should be made of "The present day and the nation," including the Constitution, the laws, their special merits and moral characteristics. This study should be plentifully illustrated by references to current literature and by visits to places that have an historical importance.

PRACTICAL CONSIDERATIONS

The realization of such a far-reaching scheme can only be achieved by slow degrees. Any child who has attended the elementary school may be admitted, not only the pupils of special schools. The school is intended for normal children, but those who are slow or backward, suffering from some psychological maladjustment (mental barriers, timidity) may be admitted with the certainty that they will benefit and show real improvement. Their number

should, however, constitute a feasible fraction of the whole community.

Boys and girls may be accommodated in one hostel: but in this
case its management should be given to a married couple, house-
father and house-mother, who would develop a moral and protec-
tive influence on the conduct of the children.

A large estate, possibly including woods or near to the sea,
would be the most suitable place. A number of teachers should be
allowed to live in the school in return for taking part in directing the
daily work of the institution. Strict discipline in everything that
effects the daily life and the aims of the school must be enforced on
the staff attached to the school as well as on the students who will
then only learn to adjust themselves to the demands of an *ordered*
environment. This means that the staff must take the responsibility
for maintaining order until the order of voluntary self-discipline is
established.

There must also be young visiting teachers, men and women
who come to give lessons. They should have the proper qualifica-
tion for teaching in secondary schools, but this does not mean that
they should be free to use their own methods, for they must agree to
adopt special methods and cooperate in the experiment. Therefore
these teachers should be young and open-minded, ready to take
part in a new experiment and ready to make their own personal
contributions. There should not be too many, rather the minimum
number who can undertake a group of related subjects, which can
be subsequently separated according to the needs of the school.

Besides the teachers of ordinary subjects there must also be
technical instructors. For instance, an instructor for agriculture and
gardening, a business manager for the shop and the hotel, and a
handicraft teacher. Other members of the staff must be specially
qualified in practical work, in cooking, or sewing and mending,
and should include an intelligent handyman capable of giving
instruction in various trades while he helps in the daily work. So
that just as the children in our elementary schools have already
learned to fold their clothes, and to sew, etc., so here they must
learn "to put things right" when necessary, to adjust a machine or

the engine of a car, to mend a broken window or the catch of a door. They should also be able to make a path, build a shed, chop firewood, and so on.

It may be asked: "how are they to earn money?" This cannot be done directly, and it will always be a difficult matter for the children to make money during their training. There must be some adult workers who will start the concern, showing how the work is done, and allow the children by degrees to do their share in the organization and accounting as well as in the actual work. There should be a modern farm or a market-garden where flowers are grown for sale, and this may be taken over as a going concern. So also the shop might be started by a voluntary committee of adults, possibly the relatives of the children—an analogous organization to those that are formed for the encouragement of handicrafts. One grown-up person should take the responsibility for the organization. But the children can take turns to give real help in the work, and they will make the place attractive by their youth and happiness as well as by their industry and resourcefulness. And so the business would develop little by little through the cooperation of the parents, the instructors, and the children themselves.

C

The Function of the University

Among educational institutions we can clearly distinguish two categories of schools: one for children and adolescents, another, the university, which is meant for adults.

If we consider the natural development of the human individual, the "preparation of the organism" is completed by the end of the eighteenth year, when the age of adolescence is over. The law recognizes this physical maturity by allowing marriage at that age. At twenty one a person becomes free of guardianship and is declared to be of age.

Usually the student enters the university after his eighteenth year and remains there some two or three years after being of age. The university therefore can be said to be really a school for adults.

This purely physiological consideration concerning its students places the university in a position that is different from that of all other schools. In its constitution, however, the university shows no marked change from other schools, it is but their continuation. The student continues to follow lessons, to listen to professors, to take examinations, and, as formerly, the success of his studies depends on the marks he receives. The only difference is that university students are not strictly held to say lessons or to do homework, whereas they have been accustomed to forced work under continuous control. This means that, as at the university this control is lifted, the students study less often. Another particular pointing to the same fact is that university students enjoy very long vacations. For the rest, they continue, as in the preceding school years, to be economically dependent upon their families. It is from the point of view of the family budget that the parents watch the success of their studies as shown by promotion and good marks. The result is that at the university there are adult men who live under the same conditions as children, with the difference that their physical maturity gives rise to problems that often find their solution in a secret life of immorality.

In the Middle Ages the university bore a stamp of grandeur and dignity. There were centers of studies such as the famous University of Bologna, to which students came from the different countries of Europe and the different Italian states.

The students had a feeling of intellectual responsibility towards their own nation or state that, in its turn, was proud to be able to count among the students of the university some of its citizens. The University of Bologna put upon the walls of its Aula Magna, richly reproduced in enamel and gold, the coats of arms of the cities and states represented by its different students.

The students took part in philosophical and political discussions that encouraged them to realize their own values and moral responsibility. The great learning and renown of the professors—their ermine cloaks, the solemn functions—were a permanent proof of the special dignity of those centers. At those universities there were no examinations except the academic one that conferred the degree. The students pursued their studies with intensity, urged to acquire the treasures of knowledge, and hoarded their years of study, taking full advantage of every hour. The festivals at the universities, which bore the stamp of art, were public events.

The universities were then, in reality, the "centers of culture" from which civilization was transmitted all over the world, the students becoming its propagators.

But today universities are not the only centers from which culture emanates. Today civilization and culture are spread everywhere by other means, which become always more extensive and easy. Culture expands through the press and other rapid communications that bring about a universal levelling.

So, the universities have gradually become ordinary professional schools, distinguishing themselves from other schools only by their more advanced culture. But they have lost the dignity and distinction that made them a central instrument of progress and civilization. Students whose aim is merely to reach a simple and obscure personal position can no longer feel that lofty mission towards an ever-greater progress of humanity that once formed the "spirit of the university." The common object of the students has become that of evading work as much as possible. Their principal aim is almost exclusively that of passing examinations anyhow and of taking the degree that will serve their individual interest. So, while there has been a progress in culture so great as to transform civil life, the universities themselves have suffered a decline. The real centers of progress today are the laboratories of scientific research, open to a very limited number and far removed from the level of common culture.

Schools today are generally felt to be in decline not because the culture given is inferior, but because the schools no longer correspond in their organization to the needs of the present time and stay below the level achieved by civilization. The latter, today, has so changed its material bases that it is really the beginning of a new civilization, while the life of man has not yet found its adaption to the new conditions.

This is what renders so critical the present period of human history. The problems of a reform of education today lie in finding the means to render possible the new adaptation which is needed.

Education should not limit itself to seeking new methods for a mostly arid transmission of knowledge: its aim must be to give the necessary aid to human development. This world, marvellous in its power, needs a "new man." It is therefore the life of man and his values that must be considered. If "the formation of man" becomes the basis of education, then the coordination of all schools from infancy to maturity, from nursery to university, arises as a first necessity: for man is a unity, an individuality that passes through interdependent phases of development. Each preceding phase prepares the one that follows, forms its base, nurtures the energies that urge towards the succeeding period of life.

The lack of coordination between the successive stages of education is resented as an obstacle in the schools even as they are today.

Universities have their own scheme of studies; they find however that the pupils of secondary schools are not sufficiently prepared to follow it. Secondary schools find themselves in the same situation in regard to the pupils coming from elementary schools, and so they all feel the burden of an unprepared individuality.

This is the case in the field of culture. But if the aim of education becomes that of achieving the development of the human personality rather than the narrower one of providing culture only, then a close coordination embracing all periods of life becomes even more essential and indispensible. Our experience with children in elementary schools has shown us that the age between six and twelve years is a period of life during which the elements of all sciences should be given. It is a period that, psychologically, is especially sensitive and might be called the "sensitive period of culture" during which the abstract plane of the human mind is organized.

It is then that everything should be sown.

This interesting period in the organization of the human soul could be compared to a field where the seed of all those plants that one wishes to flourish in the future must be sown. The aim of education must be that of finding all the possible means to "plant the seeds" in the suitable epoch. Not only secondary schools, but also universities must interest themselves in this sowing, even if the interest in lower schools is felt to be out of their realm. There is nothing that is apparently further removed from the peaceful life of the fields than the mechanical bustle and clanking of the machinery of a factory, yet the cloth manufacturer must interest himself in the planting of the flax, otherwise it would be useless to have good manufacturing implements, because the raw material would be lacking.

Thus it is with psychic life: there are special epochs when an inner activity lays in the soul the roots of the first intellectual development, calling forth enthusiastic response and awakening possibilities that otherwise would remain dormant. And these centers of keen interest that urge towards progress through vivacious activity will be developed during the rest of youth. But, if on the other hand the germs of knowledge have not been sown in the proper season, the possibilities remain dormant, inertia and emptiness persist, the individual resents all forms of intellectual effort, and study deteriorates.

The failure to consider these special epochs is a sin against the laws of life. Work becomes an arid effort, a condemnation similar to that of Adam described in the Bible. Evidently it is not work, but work against nature that is condemned by the divine curse. Study, such as it is today, is a work against nature, so the students carry it out aridly and under compulsion without animation. A supreme encouragement and a radiant light would be necessary to call forth those souls that by now are crippled by inertia and error. But this cannot be accomplished by that arid type of school which considers the personality of the student so much below his real values, and continues to increase his discouragement and inertia.

It is clear then, that even for culture, even for the purely intellectual fact of learning, the different categories of schools have a common interest. Or perhaps it would be better to say that higher schools must be interested in determining the way in which human energies are prepared in the lower ones.

When this is not the case the university professors will always find themselves confronted by minds repelling whatever is presented to them, by indifference and inertia, by restless youths who must forcibly be kept together like chained goatlings. If the path of normality is followed and the university takes an interest in the preparation given in the lower schools, then the pupils will become ardent apostles, intelligent critics, and almost cooperators with their professors.

As we said, this is true for intellectual education, but cooperation is still more necessary if one wishes to prepare not only the intellect, but the human personality in its totality. Human life cannot be fulfilled only by culture.

If one considers the question, acquisition of culture includes the idea of receptiveness. But life is not all receptiveness; rather it is an active and expansive energy that endeavours to realize its own creation on an external environment. In other words, merely to study is not to live, but to live is the most essential condition in order to be able to study.

We have seen this also in our experiments. Culture, which has been given anyhow and anyhow taken and assimilated, does not satisfy the human personality. Other needs exist, which if not satisfied always cause inner conflicts that influence the mental state and confuse the clarity of the mind.

Joy, feeling one's own value, being appreciated and loved by others, feeling useful and capable of production are all factors of enormous value for the human soul. It is in its eventual action on these human factors and not only in the giving of culture that the new university should find a renewed dignity and importance in relation to civilization.

In former times universities were based on a moral and philosophical conception of life and of the "mission of man." Culture was then the splendid means given to humanity so that it could reach higher levels. Today, however, it is not by philosophizing nor by discussing metaphysical conceptions that the morals of mankind can be developed: it is by activity, by experience, and by action. It is interesting to notice how attractive all practical actions become even during the period of development that precedes adolescence.

Being active with one's own hands, having a determined practical aim to reach, is what really gives inner discipline. When the hand perfects itself in a work chosen spontaneously and the will to succeed is born together with the will to overcome difficulties or obstacles; it is then that something which differs from intellectual learning arises. The realization of one's own value is born in the consciousness.

It is surprising to notice that even from the earliest age man finds the greatest satisfaction in feeling independent. The exalting feeling of being sufficient to oneself comes as a revelation. This is undoubtedly a fundamental element of social life, because when one is completely dependent upon others and the feeling of one's practical incapacity has become a conviction, the urge cannot arise to be of help or to seek the cooperation of others to act with one's own energy.

In short, self-valuation and the ability to take part in a social organization form a live force. This moral construction cannot be acquired merely by learning by heart some lessons or by solving problems that have nothing to do with one's own life. Culture must be the means, for nothing shows the necessity of culture more clearly than finding by experience how essential it is in order to live consciously and intelligently, when it is life itself and not culture that is the center around which education revolves. Culture acquires, then, great attractiveness.

To become conscious of the essential help given by it, to feel how indispensable it is to achieve perfection, success, and therefore the joy of the spirit; this is the greatest urge to study.

It is this relation between life and culture that has enabled us to understand that children can learn much more than the schools of today ask of them by their curricula, and that it is in childhood that it is necessary to arouse the first interest, to sow the seed of all sciences.

A person grows as a unity and if the development of an essential part is lacking, troubling complexes arise in the soul and in the mind.

The realization of one's own value is just the thing that urges to association, because he who is conscious of his values is victorious over life. He is an energy. We have been able to see that association arises spontaneously even when it is merely a case of thinking and of understanding. It seems that the capacity of really understanding is connected with discussion, with criticism, or with assent of others. The satisfaction of knowing must be immediately communicated to others, and in this communication enthusiasm increases. True study and thinking require the same association as is required by manual work. It was always realized that anyone who does work that is too hard must join together with others; but we saw among small children that even to be able to understand it is necessary to join with others. Spontaneous collaboration in all manifestations of life is a fact that has come as a true revelation. Association gives new strength by stimulating the energies. To act in association with others either in thought or in practice is the only way in which the human nature can be active. All this shows clearly that education cannot be kept within the limits of a closed room in which the student remains inert and always dependent upon the teacher while being kept separate from his fellow students. An education so limited is insufficient even for children.

The first reform in education must be to offer a wider environment and to multiply the possibilites of association and of activity. It is during the period of adolescence that interest in the construction and functioning of society presents itself in germinal form in the individual consciousness. Now, society is built up by various activities and not only by purely intellectual ones. The greatest element in its construction is the growing sentiment of the conscience of the individual, which develops through and by means of social experiences.

The inert child who never worked with his hands, who never had the feeling of being useful and capable of effort, who never found by experience that to live means living socially, and that to think and to create means to make use of a harmony of souls; this type of child will become a selfish youth, he will be pessimistic and melancholy and will seek on the surface of vanity the compensation for a lost paradise.

And thus, a lessened man, he will appear at the gates of the university. And to ask for what? . . . To ask for a profession that will render him capable of making his home in a society in which he is a stranger and which is indifferent to him. He will enter into society in order to take part in the functioning of a civilization for which he lacks all feeling.

No, it is not possible to take the human being into consideration only when he is a man, the human individual must be taken into consideration much before. He who one day wants to see before him a man, must first have sought the child. To detach the various phases of life is absolutely absurd.

The adult is the result of a child. Every adult is the achievement of a grown-up child; the causes of good or of evil in the adult must all be sought in the very short period of the child's growth.

The separation made between the interests of the child and those of the adult, both in education and in social questions, reminds me of a dispute which took place in the Middle Ages between two cities that possessed notable relics: one had the skulls of the Three Wise Men of the East when children; the other had the skulls of the Three Wise Men of the East when adults.

This fatal criterion, this kind of psychic barrier that neatly separates the two interests, causes grave errors and gives rise to dangers that affect the whole of civilized humanity. Among the means eminently capable of defending the safety of the people against threatening dangers, no consideration whatsoever is given to strengthening and straightening humanity by all possible means when it is still in the formative period.

What our marvellous civilization lacks today is the strength of the spiritual man, the straightness of conscience that feels its responsibility, but above all the feeling that human life is triumphant over the cosmos: humankind should feel itself king of all that has been created, transformer of the earth, builder of a new nature, collaborator in the universal work of creation.

He who arrives at the university has left behind him childhood and adolescence: he is a formed person. A great part of his social destiny, of the success of his studies will depend on how he was formed.

What interests him now is the "mission of humankind."

He should certainly not be limited to the acquisition of that knowledge which will be necessary for him in the exercise of his profession. University students are adults, who will be called upon to exercise an influence upon the civilization of their times.

From the universities educators, therefore the guides of the new generation, the leaders of the new humanity emerge. From the universities come those men who will be called to lead the masses and to defend civilization.

When they take their examinations to get their degrees they will be facing the gates of the world, and must possess a great moral preparation. They did not remain at school after they had already become adults merely in order to acquire a little more knowledge than others. Culture forms a great part of their preparation, it is true, but they could have found culture all around them, for today culture has pervaded the entire social environment. The functions of the university would be to intensify it and to make it penetrate into the conscience as a weapon for the defense of humanity and of civilization.

As there is a religion for all—though priests and missionaries possess a religion more intensely penetrating, a religion that creates action in favor of mankind—so is culture spread everywhere and has reached the same level among all civilized people—though some select men partake of it more profoundly and become its apostles in order to preserve civilization.

Also, in the university preparation could be more extensive. If it is true that even for children education cannot be carried out within the four walls of the school, so much more this must be repeated for adults. It is necessary even for a child to feel himself independent: the adult must then have already realized his independence.

The social experience begun earlier must be continued, because the person who has never worked, who has never tried to make his own living, who has never mingled with people of different age and of different social classes, will with difficulty become worthy of becoming the leader of anything. This "value of the personality" must have been nurtured by each individual through active efforts and positive experiences.

It is certainly not by philosophizing or by meditating only that the conscience of modern man will be formed.

As regards culture, it is in the very character of the university to "learn how to study." The degree is but the proof of knowing how to study, of how to seek culture alone and without help, of being set upon the path of scientific research. This is another proof that the essential task of the university is not limited to giving instruction. It is in order to study, that one has learned to study.

An individual who has taken his degree has acquired a better knowledge of how to sail upon the ocean of culture that has flooded the world. He has but received an orientation. Therefore he is a studious person who possesses a compass that allows him to enter into communication with the stars that direct the way.

Such is the person who has taken a degree. And if the degree, as far as its value is concerned, is but the capacity for studying, why then should study at the university be limited to three or six years? One who studies at the university knows already that he will have to study all his life or lose his value. Why then so much bustle, during those few years, for the acquisition of culture that will have no end? There must be another kind of formative help, an effort to become keenly aware of the needs of one's own time and to permeate oneself with civilization.

It will be of great advantage for a really studious individual to begin to conquer economic independence during the period of his university studies. Many a young person, while he attends the university, is already a private teacher, or a journalist, an artist or a merchant, and even a common workman or a waiter. Many have already situations in broadcasting companies or in diplomacy.

These workers are more likely to study for the love of study and of human progress, and not for the immediate and direct purpose of a profession. If they take one or two years longer in their studies, what does it matter? Considering that their study will never cease, why should they take so much trouble to obtain in the shortest possible time the advantages that the degree affords them; when they are destined, if they wish to keep up with the ever-rising level of efficiency, to pursue the new things that are continuously being elaborated in the field of their profession?

One can study while one works to make one's living. All those who wish to become university professors do it. They go on studying, but they do not go to school. They make a modest living just to be able to study and reach higher levels in the future. They even marry and have a family that will later attain a high social position.

An adult who studies must not be worried as a child by examinations, nor fear the scoldings of a father who is forced to support him by what little means he possesses. He should not resort to subterfuges in order to get good marks, nor dishonor himself because he cannot keep chaste.

A university student must first of all know how to achieve his own independence and moral equilibrium.

I believe that all possible provision should be made in order to create some form of work to confer economic independence on the students of the university so that each may really be free to study and be able to find his own place in accordance with his own value.

I shall finish by comparing the life of the human being to the three stages of the life of Christ.

Behold at first the miraculous and sublime Child.

This epoch is the period of "creative sensibilities," of mental construction, of such an intense activity that it is necessary to sow in this period of life all the seeds of culture.

Then comes the epoch of adolescence, an epoch of inner revelations and of social sensibilities. Christ as a boy, forgetful of His family, is heard to discuss with the doctors. He does not talk as a pupil, but as a Teacher, dazzling by the flashes of His light. But later He devotes Himself to manual work and exercises a craft. He shows that the adolescent should be able to manifest his hidden treasures and at the same time work and be initiated into a craft.

At last, comes the Man Who prepares Himself for His mission in this world.

And what does He do for this preparation?

He confronts the Evil One and overpowers him. This is the preparation!

Each human being possesses the strength of becoming aware of, and of facing the dangers, the temptations of the world so as to become inured to them in order to overcome them.

The temptations to be overcome are literally those illustrated in the Gospel: the temptation of possession and the temptation of power.

There is something in humankind that stands above them: it is able to understand what is required to create a very powerful, a very rich, and a purified world.

There is only one way: that each individual know how to overcome the temptations of power and possession.

That is the path of his kingdom.

But in order to attain this level through education, it is necessary to seek the child and to consider him under a new aspect.

Index

Abstract
  child's world of the, 23–24, 36
  education, passage from sen-
    sorial to, 11, 19, 33–40
  thinking, need for, 11
Academic materials, 24
Actions, practical, 128
Activity (child's), 134
  depending on favorable condi-
    tions, 10
  diginity in, 18
  external, 25
  growth through physical, 18
  guidance of, 113
  long hikes, 18
  motor, 12
  need for abstraction and intel-
    lectual, 11
  preserving equilibrium between
    acting and thinking, 24
  scouting, 29
Acts of courtesy, 17
Adaptability, 99
Adolescence, period of, 4
Adolescent
  alternating studies with practi-
    cal life, 120
  characteristics of, 101–2
  diet of, 114
  economic independence of, 102
  history for, 118

importance of independence for, 133
period, first, 114
physical conditions of, 114
physical and emotional problems of, 101
reforms relating to needs of,
  102–109
requirements of the, 112–14
schools not adapted to, 97
syllabus and methods for, 115–19
Adult
  causes of good and evil in, 131
  child's means of freeing himself
    from, 23–24
  creating environment for child's
    changing needs, 25–26
  educating the child on the ab-
    stract plane, 25, 39
  facilitating child's mobility, 26
Age (child's)
  characteristics of different, 3–4
  chronological subdivisions, 4
  metamorphoses due to changing,
    5, 9–10
  needs peculiar to each, 112
  of adolescence, 134
  of interior revelations, 134
  of social sensitivities, 134
Agriculture, 106
  teacher of, 120
Alphabet, letters as symbols, 68

Anatomy, comparative, 117
Anomalies, development of, 10
Arts, 115
Association, among children as
    aid to learning, 130
Astronomy, 117
Attention, concentration of, 62

"Bad marks," 100
Bible, the, 127
Bicycle, safety and maintenance, 25
Biology, 117
Body (child's), 114
Bookkeeping, 109
Botany, 117
Buying objects, by child, 9

Care of self, 27–28
Chemistry
    experiments, 59–64
    inorganic, 77–79, 85
    Organic, 83–90
Child
    awareness of the value of
        money by, 9
    care of the personality of, 100–
        101
    conditions favoring, 10
    conforming to the rules of
        scouting, 18
    conscience of, 12–13
    coordination of the movement
        of, 18
    difficulties due to the vital
        needs of, 102
    finding correlation between
        things with, 93
    imagination of, 38
    independent thinking of, 17, 105
    intellectual plane of, 11, 29
    living two parallel existences, 28
    metamorphosis, physical and
        psychic, of, 5, 9–13
    mobility of, 26
    moral characteristics from 7 to
        12 years, 17–19
    needs from 7 to 12 years, 17–19
    precision, requirement of, 38
    "rebirth" of, 3

"Children's Houses," 104–5, 112
Christ, 112, 134
Classification
    as outline for study, 39, 50
    by means of the senses, 11
Clothes, importance of, 26, 28
Collaboration, 130
Color, 3, 82
Comenius, 33–34
Commitment of individual to
    group, 19. See also Scouting
Consent of child, 19
Control of error, 127
Coordination
    between phases of nursery to
        university, 126
    of movement of the child, 17
"Creative sensitivity," 134
Culture, 132
    sensitive period for, 126

Daily living exercises. See Exercises
D'Annunzio, Gabriel, 25
Degree, 133
Dental hygiene, 25
Detail
    importance of study, 39–40, 93
    meditation on, 35
Diction, exercises in, 115
Diet, 114
Dignity, child's sense of, 18
Discipline, 123
    as aspect of individual liberty, 113
    through manual work, 128
Discovery of reality, 25
"Distributive justice," principle of,
    12–13

Economic independence, 102
Education
    essential principle of, 94
    for laborers, 99
    for liberty and independence of, 25
    importance of moral, 12, 18
    passage from sensorial to ab-
        stract, 11, 38
    physical, 113–14
    purpose "formation of man," 125
    reform of, 130

relationship between life and, 129
role of, 24
sports introduced in, 100
successive levels of, 3–5
Educator. *See* Teacher
Environment
assimilation of, 53, 71
for 7 to 12 year olds, 9–10
for adolescents, 105–7
reaction to inadequate, 10
Equality, 12
Erdkinder, 97, 107–8
Evolvement of the individual, 3
Exercises
aim of, 18
artistic, 115
imagination, 115
importance of, 25, 35
language, 115
practical life, 17, 25, 104–5
Sensorial. *See* Sensorial materials
technical and scientific, 59–60
Expression, personal, 115
Exterior world, child's preference
for, 11

Faith, in God and oneself, 102
Fantasy, 37
Feet and legs, care of, 25
Fish, study of life of, 51
"Formation of man," 125
Free choice, 113
Freedom of the child, emphasized, 19

Genesis, 36
Geography, 49
Geology, 117
Good and Evil, problems of, 12, 131
Gospel, the, 135
Group, individual's commitment
to, 19
Growth of the child, 3

Hair, care of, 25
Hands, value of work with, 128, 130
Heat, study of, 44
History
aids in studying, 118–119
facets of, 118–119

Home environment. *See* Environment
Hotel, 107–8
Hygiene, 25

Ideals, 93
Imagination, 33–40
science as stimulating the, 64
Independence, 17, 24, 102, 133
in thinking of 7 to 12 year olds,
23
Individual
improvement of the, 98
rights, 12
Inertia, 127
Information, acquisition of, 25
Initiative, as leading to self-disci-
pline, 113
Injustice, concept of, 12–13
Inner activity, as roots of intel-
lectual development, 127
Insects, 3, 34
Insecurity, caused by modern con-
ditions, 98
Instruction, brought to life, 23
Intellectual activity, 11–12
obstacles to, 36
Intellectual capacity, diminution
of, 101
Intellectual professions, 99
Intelligence, study and, 112
Interest, 63
Introduction to reading. *See* Read-
ing aloud

Jesus, 112, 134
Judgment of acts, 12
Justice, concept of, 12

Knowledge
by means of pictures and objects, 33
inertia in aquisition of, 127

Language, exercises, 115
Learning, aided by association
with children, 130
Lyon, Mary, 103

Machines, significance of, 117–18

Mankind, 102, 118
Manual work, 103, 128, 130. *See also* Training
Mathematics, 93, 116
  helping the imagination, 43, 45
  understanding of, through experimentation, 43–44, 55
Meditation on detail, 34
Mental health, 36
Metamorphosis, 9–13
Mind
  abstract structure of, 11, 93
  constructed to an exact plan, 11
  mathematical and philosophical, 93
Mineralogy, study of, 49
Money, 9
  bookkeeping, 109
  earned by adolescents, 103
Moral education, 116
Moral problems, interest in, 12
Moral relationships, development of, 18
Museums, in schools, 34, 117
Music, 115

Nature
  as subject matter for instruction, 34, 45, 67–73
  inadequate education suppressing child's, 10
  intimate movements of, 73
  of creation, 88
"Naughtiness," 10

Obedience, 18
Observations, importance of children's, 29, 47, 49
Occupation, value of change in, 114
Orbis Sensualism Pictus, 33
Outdoors
  activities, learning from, 25–36
  life in, 117

Pedagogy, 34
Perception. *See* Sensorial exercises
Philosophy, 93
Physics, principles of, 49
Physiology, 117

Pictures, knowledge by means of, 33
Playthings, 117
Poetry, 53, 68
Practical exercises, 25, 120
Precision, requirement of, 38
Preparation for tasks, importance of, 26, 28
Primitive logic, use of, 64
Progress
  made by science, 97
  studies relating to human, 117–18
Psychic entity of the child, 10–11
Puberty, 98

Quantities, idea of, 43

Reality, discovering of, 26, 34
Regression, 10
Religion, 119, 132
Repetition, 17
Research, desire for, 93
Rewards, 12
Right, concept of, 12
Rigors, regimen of, 19
Rules, 115

Saint Francis of Assisi, 53
School
  as preparation for life, 11
  boarding, 104
  closed, insufficient for child, 10
  elementary, 124
  of social life, experimental, 102
  secondary, 106–7
    failure of, 100
    reform of, 99–100
  "self-help," 104
Science
  as speaking to the imagination, 53, 64
  practical applications of, 97
  progress made by, 97
Scouting
  activities, 29
  as organized activity for children, 11
  moral aim of, 18
  obedience in, 18
  rigors and rules, 18

studying animal tracks in, 29
useful elements in, 29
voluntary nature of, 18
Self, care and inspection of, 27–8
Self-confidence, need to fortify, 102
Self-discipline. *See* Discipline
Self-expression, 115
Senses, absorbing exterior world
 by, 11
Sensitive period for culture, 126
Sensorial exercises
 by contact with nature, 35
 tactile, 38
 visual, 34–35
Sensorial level of education, 11
Silence lesson, 62
Social experience, 17, 27, 132
 blended with environment, 26
 moral teachings sought through, 26
 schools providing opportunity
  for, 106
Social organization, 129
Social relations, 26
Society
 classes of, 105
 reforms relating to the present,
  102–5
 relationship to, 10, 129
Specialization, 98, 111
Sports, 100
Stoppani, Antonio, 45
Store, run by children, 125
Studies
 program of, 113
Study
 and work plans, 111–14
 as meditation on detail, 34
"Supernatural" powers, 118
Symbols
 letters of the alphabet as, 68
 musical notes as, 68
 of life, activities constituting, 29

Teachers
 for practical work, 120
 limitations of, 24
 on special subjects, 120
 qualifications for, 120

Tobacco, use of, 114
Training, self-activity
 by drawing, 115
 by intellectual work, 103
 by manual work (occupations), 103
 by observation, 49–50
 by observing objects in museums, 34
 by participation in social organizations, 129
 by pictures, 33
 by sports, 100
 by study of animals, vegetables,
  and minerals, 39
 by study of aquatic shells, 48
 by study of corals, 48
 by study of fish, 51
 by swimming, 27
 by using machines, 117
 by visits to historic places, 119

Universe, child's understanding of
 the, 36
University
 decadence of modern, 125
 degree, meaning of, 133
 function of the, 123–35
 in the Middle Ages, 124
 preparation at the, 132
 studies, achieving financial independence during, 133–34
 treatment of students, 123–24

Walking, 25
Water, 43–55
Work
 group, 115
 importance of, 103–5
 individual, 115
 manual, aiding inner discipline,
  128, 130
 not fatiguing, 105
 rural, as approach to scientific
  and historic studies, 106
 teaching economic independence, 104

Zoology, 117